सीताराम

Hanuman Chalisa Legacy Book
Endowment of Devotion

Embellish it with Your
Rama Namas
& Present it to Someone You Love

हनुमान चालीसा व राम-नाम माला

Belongs to _____

Presented to _____
_____

Published by: only **RAMA** only
(an Imprint of e1i1 Corporation)

Title: Hanuman Chalisa Legacy Book - Endowment of Devotion
Sub-Title: Embellish it with your Rama Namas & present it to someone you love

Author/Designer: Sushma

Parts of this book have been derived/inspired from our other publication:
"Rama Hymns" (Authored by Sushma)

Copyright Notice: **Copyright © e1i1 Corporation © Sushma**
All rights reserved. No part of this publication may be reproduced, distributed, or transmitted in any form or by any means, including photocopying, recording, or other electronic or mechanical methods.

Identifiers
ISBN: **978-1-945739-27-9** (Paperback)
ISBN: **978-1-945739-94-1** (Hardcover)
—o—

—o—
www.e1i1.com -- www.OnlyRama.com
email: e1i1*books*e1i1@gmail.com

Our books can be bought online, or at Amazon, or any bookstore. If a book is not available at your neighborhood bookstore they will be happy to order it for you. (Certain Hardcover Editions may not be immediately available—we apologize) Some of our Current/Forthcoming Books are listed below. Please note that this is a partial list and that we are continually adding new books. Please visit www.**e1i1**.com / www.**onlyRama**.com for current offerings.

- **Tulsi Ramayana—The Hindu Bible:** Ramcharitmanas with English Translation & Transliteration
- **Ramcharitmanas:** Ramayana of Tulsidas with Transliteration (in English)
- **Ramayana, Large**: Tulsi Ramcharitmanas, Hindi only Edition, Large Font and Paper size
- **Ramayana, Medium**: Tulsi Ramcharitmanas, Hindi only Edition, Medium Font and Paper size
- **Ramayana, Small**: Tulsi Ramcharitmanas, Hindi only Edition, Small Font and Paper size
- **Sundarakanda**: The Fifth-Ascent of Tulsi Ramayana
- **Bhagavad Gita, The Holy Book of Hindus:** Original Sanskrit Text with English Translation & Transliteration
- **Bhagavad Gita (Sanskrit):** Original Sanskrit Text with Transliteration – No Translation –
- **My Bhagavad Gita Journal:** Journal for recording your everyday thoughts alongside the Bhagavad Gita
- **RAMA GOD:** In the Beginning - Upanishad Vidya (Know Thyself)
- **Purling Shadows:** And A Dream Called Life - Upanishad Vidya (Know Thyself)
- **Rama Hymns:** Hanuman-Chalisa, Rama-Raksha-Stotra, Bhushumdi-Ramayana, Nama-Ramayanam, Rama-Shata-Nama-Stotra, etc. with Transliteration & English Translation
- **Rama Jayam - Likhita Japam :: Rama-Nama Mala** (several): Rama-Nama Journals for Writing the 'Rama' Name 100,000 Times
- **Tulsi-Ramayana Rama-Nama Mala** (multiple volumes): Legacy Journals for Writing the Rama Name alongside Tulsi Ramayana
- **Legacy Books - Endowment of Devotion** (multiple volumes): Legacy Journals for Writing the Rama Name alongside Sacred Hindu Texts

कलिजुग केवल हरि गुन गाहा । गावत नर पावहिं भव थाहा ॥
kalijuga kevala hari guna gāhā, gāvata nara pāvahiṁ bhava thāhā.
कलिजुग जोग न जग्य न ग्याना । एक अधार राम गुन गाना ॥
kalijuga joga na jagya na gyānā, eka adhāra rāma guna gānā.

The only appointed means for the Kali-Yuga is singing the praises of the Lord—and just following that simple path, people are able to cross this turbulent worldly life. In this Yuga neither Yoga nor Yagya nor Wisdom is of much avail—the only hope is in chanting the Holy-Name राम राम राम.

In all the four ages; in all times, past, present, or future; in the three spheres of creation—any creature that repeats the name राम becomes blessed. The name of Rāma is like the tree of paradise, and is the centre of all that is good in the world, and whoever meditates upon it verily becomes transformed—from vile to holy. As Narasingh became manifest to destroy Hiranyākashyap, the enemy of heaven, in order to protect Prahlād—so is the Name of Rāma राम, for the destruction of the wicked and the protection of the pious.

The chanting of Rāma-Nāma is a direct way to liberation. By repeating the राम name—whether in joy or in sadness, in activity or in repose—bliss is diffused all around. According to the Vedas, just as the Sun dispels darkness, the chanting of Rāma-Nāma dispels all the evils and obstacles of life. The Rāma Nāma cures agony and showers the blessings of God; all righteous wishes get fulfilled; jealousy and pride disappear; life becomes imbued with satisfaction and peace; all of life's needs fall in place automatically—just like a miracle of nature guiding nature's forces. You may not always get what you want in the exact same form, but the Rāma-Nāma will purify things and bring to you the same needed happiness and bliss in a much more refined and lasting way. Life truly becomes filled with tranquility. With the Rāma-Nāma, an immense sense of inner spiritual wellbeing is experienced apart from a gain of external material happiness.

राम नाम मनिदीप धरु जीह देहरीं द्वार ।
rāma nāma manidīpa dharu jīha deharīṁ dvāra,
तुलसी भीतर बाहेरहुँ जौं चाहसि उजिआर ॥
tulasī bhītara bāherahuṁ jauṁ cāhasi ujiāra.

O Tulsīdās, place the luminous gem in the shape of the divine name 'Rāma' on the tongue—which is at the threshold, the doorway to the inside—and you will have light both on inside and outside. (i.e. Always chant राम, and its radiance will illumine your mind, body, life—all around, everywhere, inside out.)

Rāma Jayam: Journal for writing the Holy-Name राम. Once embellished with your Rāma-Nāmas, this journal will become a priceless treasure which you can present to your loved ones—an unparalleled gift of love, labor, caring, wishing, and above all—Devotion.

To write राम in Sanskrit, trace the contours 1-2 (which is the sound of **r** in '**r**un'), 3-4 (the sound **a** in '**a**rk'), 5-6 & 7-8 (the sound **m** in '**m**ust') and lastly mark the top line 9-10. Please note the pronunciation: राम rhymes with calm.

जय हनुमान

जय सीताराम

jaya
hanumāna
jaya
sītārāma

Hanuman-Chalisa

राम राम राम राम राम राम राम राम राम राम राम राम राम राम राम राम राम राम

Today's Date : _____

सीताराम
सीताराम
सीताराम सीताराम
सीताराम सीताराम
सीताराम सीताराम

ॐ

सीताराम सीताराम सीताराम सीताराम सीताराम
सीताराम सीताराम सीताराम सीताराम सीताराम
सीताराम सीताराम सीताराम सीताराम सीताराम सीताराम

श्रीजानकीवल्लभो विजयते
śrījānakīvallabho vijayate

श्री हनुमान चालीसा
śrī hanumāna cālīsā

(dohā)

śrīguru caraṇa saroja raja nija mana mukura sudhāri ,

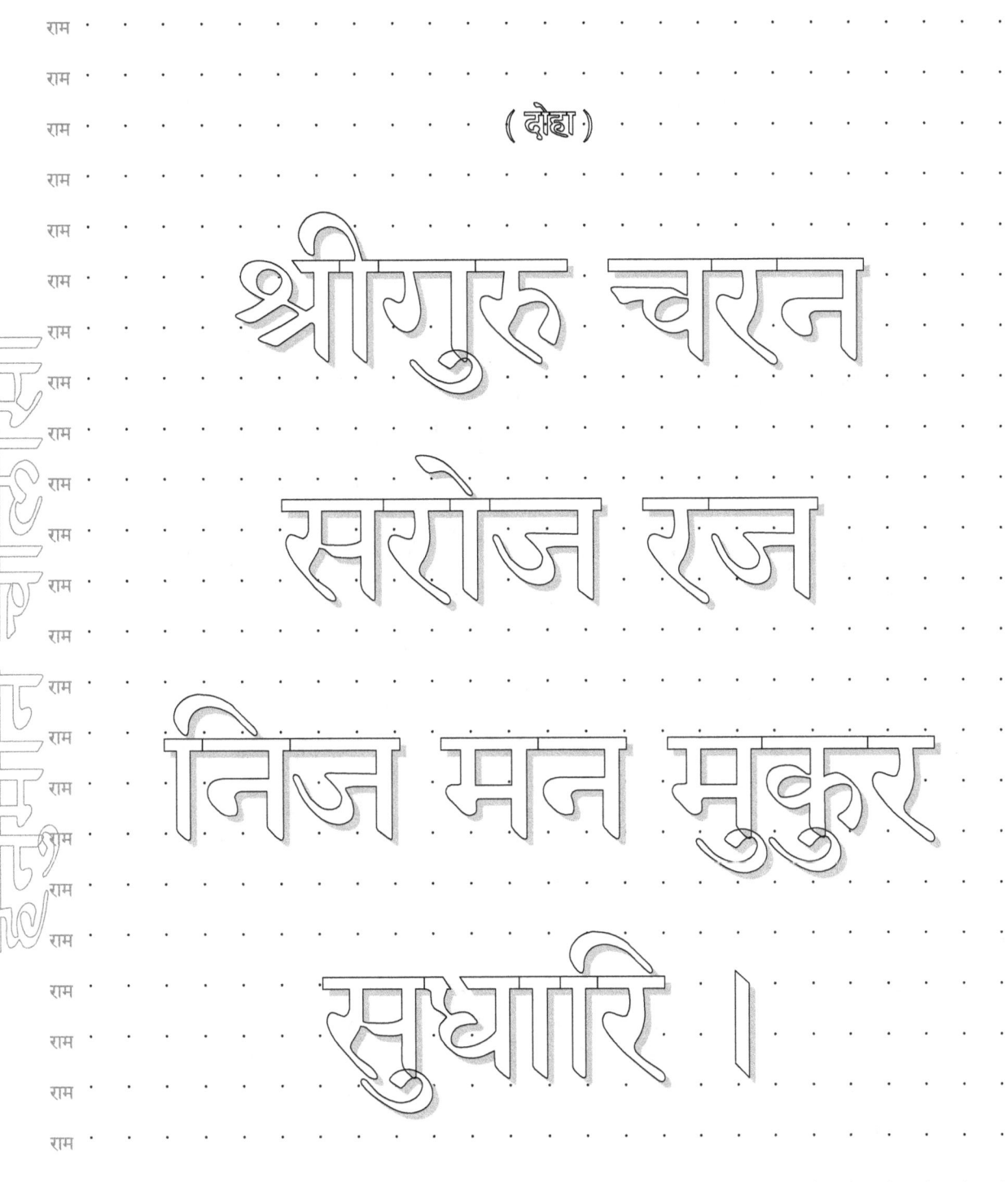

दोहा - dohā

श्रीगुरु चरन सरोज रज निज मन मुकुर सुधारि ।
śrīguru carana saroja raja nija mana mukura sudhāri,
Cleansing the mirror of my mind with the pollen dust from the lotus feet of the revered Guru,

baranaūṁ raghubara bimala jasa jo dāyaka phala cāri .

बरनउँ रघुबर बिमल जस जो दायक फल चारि ॥
baranauṁ raghubara bimala jasa jo dāyaka phala cāri.
I sing the unsullied glories of Shrī Rāma—the bestower of the four fruits of life.

buddhi hīna tanu jānikai sumiraum̐ pavana kumāra ,

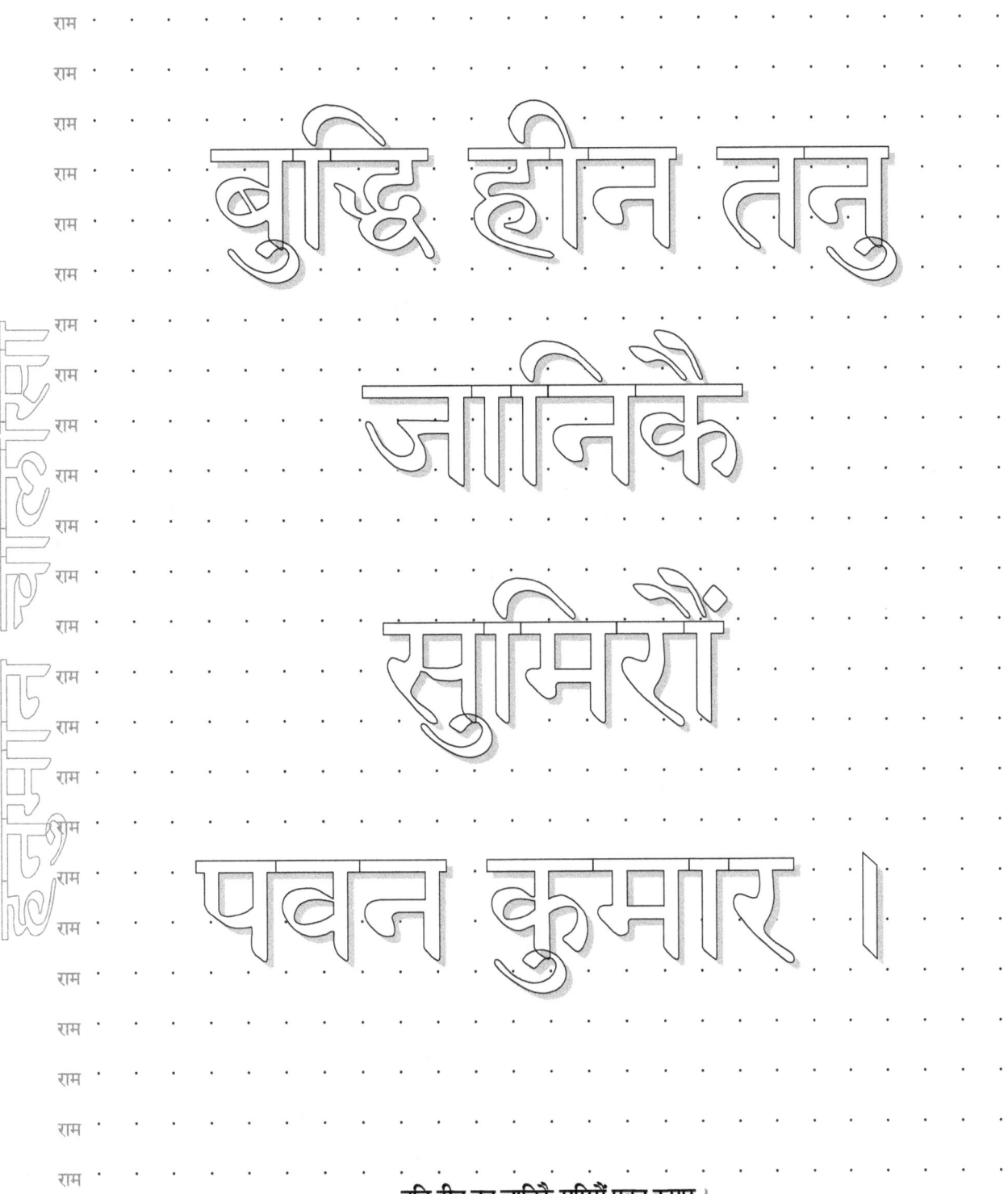

बुद्धि हीन तनु जानिकै सुमिरौं पवन कुमार ।
buddhi hīna tanu jānikai sumirauṁ pavana kumāra,
Knowing this material body to be void of intelligence and seeped in ignorance, I meditate on the Son-of-Wind seeking his favor:

bala buddhi bidyā dehu mohi harahu kaleśa vikāra .

बल बुद्धि बिद्या देहु मोहि हरहु कलेश विकार ॥
bala buddhi bidyā dehu mohi harahu kaleśa vikāra.
Impart to me strength, intelligence, virtuosity; and remove all ailments and imperfections, my Lord.

(caupāī)

jaya hanumāna jñāna guṇa sāgara ,
jaya kapīśa tihuṁ loka ujāgara .

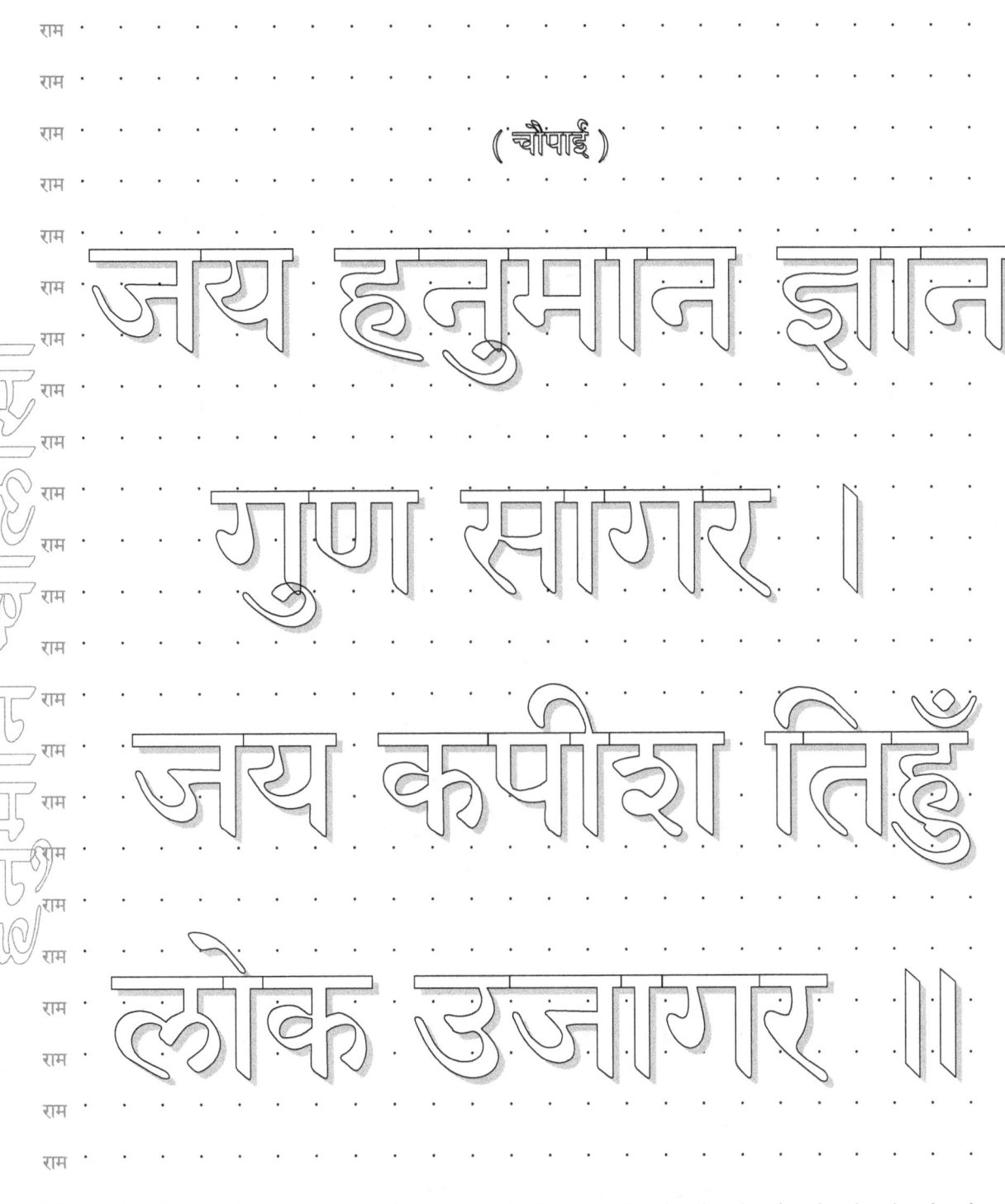

(चौपाई)

जय हनुमान ज्ञान गुण सागर ।
जय कपीश तिहुँ लोक उजागर ॥

चौपाई : caupāī

जय हनुमान ज्ञान गुण सागर । जय कपीश तिहुँ लोक उजागर ॥
jaya hanumāna jñāna guṇa sāgara, jaya kapīśa tihuṁ loka ujāgara. 1.
Glory be to Hanumān—the ocean of wisdom and virtues. Victory to the monkey-god whose resplendency irradiates the three spheres of creation.

rāma dūta atulita bala dhāmā, aṁjani-putra pavanasuta nāmā.

Hanuman-Chalisa

राम राम राम राम राम राम राम राम राम राम राम राम राम राम राम

राम दूत अतुलित बल धामा । अंजनिपुत्र पवनसुत नामा ॥
rāma dūta atulita bala dhāmā, aṁjani-putra pavanasuta nāmā. 2.
Glory be to the divine messenger and servant of Shrī Rāma, the repository of immeasurable strength. Glory be to mother Anjani's boy, bearing the name Pavana-Suth—Son-of-Wind.

mahābīra
bikrama
bajaraṁgī,
kumati
nivāra
sumati ke
saṁgī.

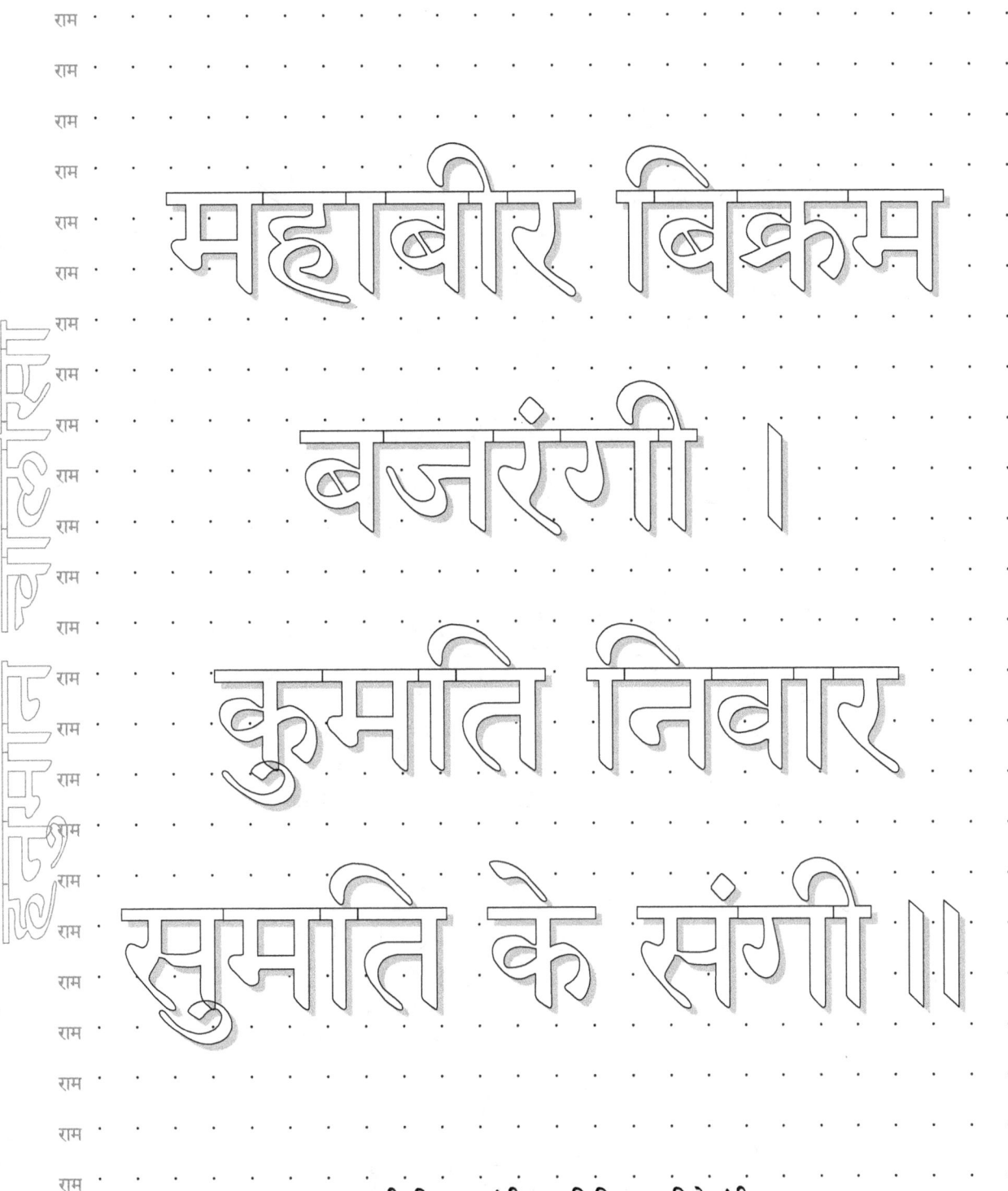

महाबीर बिक्रम बजरंगी । कुमति निवार सुमति के संगी ॥
mahābīra bikrama bajaraṁgī, kumati nivāra sumati ke saṁgī. 3.
O supremely valorous hero of wondrous great deeds, with a body that is strong as diamond:
evilness of the mind you cure; a companion you are of those with minds good and pure.

kaṁcana
baraṇa
birāja
subeṣā,
kānana
kuṁḍala
kuṁcita
keśā .

कंचन बरन बिराज सुबेषा । कानन कुंडल कुंचित केशा ॥
kaṁcana barana birāja subeṣā, kānana kuṁḍala kuṁcita keśā. 4.
With a complexion that's molten gold, you shine resplendent in your exquisite form—with rings in your ears and lovely curly locks.

hātha bajra aura dhvajā birājai, kāṁdhe mūṁja janeū sājai.

हाथ बज्र और ध्वजा बिराजै । काँधे मूँज जनेऊ साजै ॥
hātha bajra aura dhvajā birājai, kāṁdhe mūṁja janeū sājai. 5.
In your hands are held a mace and a flag; and there's *Munji* and *Janeu* embellished across your shoulders, well adorned.

śaṅkara svayaṁ keśarī naṁdana ,
teja pratāpa mahā jaga baṁdana .

शङ्कर स्वयं केशरीनंदन । तेज प्रताप महा जग बंदन ॥
śaṅkara svayaṁ keśarīnaṁdana, teja pratāpa mahā jaga baṁdana. 6.
You are Shankar himself (embodied as Hanuman), born to the mighty Keshari—the delight of his heart; your majesty and prowess is astounding—venerated throughout the universe.

vidyā-vāna guṇī ati cātura,
rāma kāja karibe ko ātura.

विद्यावान गुणी अति चातुर । राम काज करिबे को आतुर ॥
vidyā-vāna guṇī ati cātura, rāma kāja karibe ko ātura. 7.
Learned in all the sciences, virtuous, most clever and wise—you are ever so eager to do all of Rāma's work.

prabhu caritra sunibe ko rasiyā, rāma lakhana sītā mana basiyā.

प्रभु चरित्र सुनिबे को रसिया । राम लखन सीता मन बसिया ॥

prabhu caritra sunibe ko rasiyā, rāma lakhana sītā mana basiyā. 8.

Your greatest delight is in listening to the glories of the Lord, and Rāma-Lakshman-Sītā ever reside in your heart; nay—you ever abide in the hearts of Lakshman-Sītā-Rāma.

sūkṣma rūpa dhari siyahiṁ dikhāvā, bikaṭa rūpa dhari laṁka jarāvā.

सूक्ष्म रूप धरि सियहिं दिखावा । बिकट रूप धरि लंक जरावा ॥
sūkṣma rūpa dhari siyahiṁ dikhāvā, bikaṭa rūpa dhari laṁka jarāvā. 9.
When visiting mother Sītā you showed yourself in tiny diminutive form; then growing to fearsome colossal size you burnt the whole of Laṅkā down;

bhīma rūpa dhari asura saṁhāre, rāmacandra ke kāja saṁvāre.

भीम रूप धरि असुर सँहारे । रामचन्द्र के काज सँवारे ॥
bhīma rūpa dhari asura saṁhāre, rāma-candra ke kāja saṁvāre. 10.
assuming a valorous form you destroyed many demons—thus you ever serve to facilitate the works of the Lord-God Shrī Rāma-Chandra.

lāya saṁjīvani lakhana jiyāye, śrī raghubīra haraṣi ura lāye.

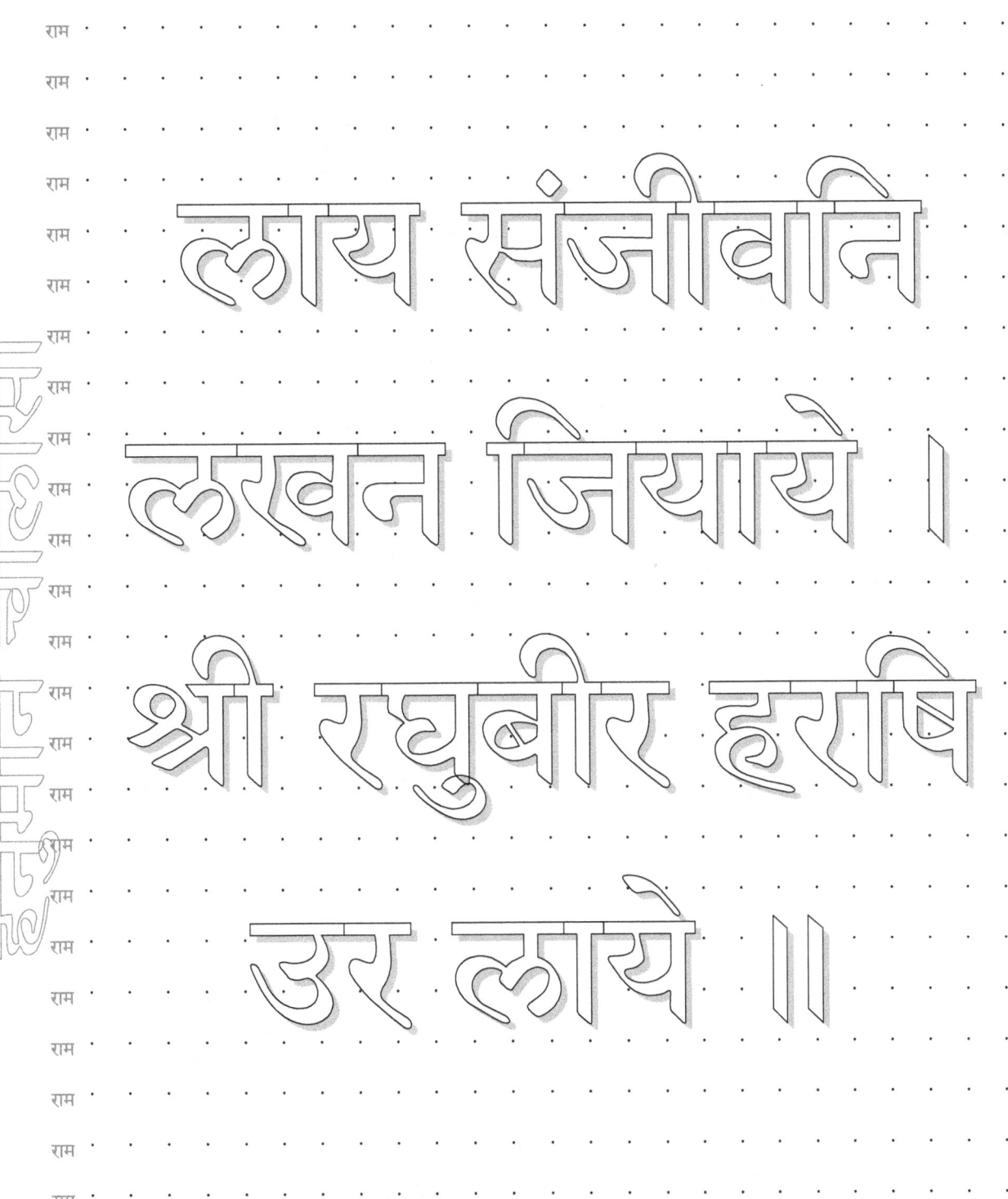

लाय संजीवनि लखन जियाये । श्री रघुबीर हरषि उर लाये ॥
lāya samjīvani lakhana jiyāye, śrī raghu-bīra haraṣi ura lāye. 11.
You brought the *Sanjīvani* and brought Lakshman back to life—whereupon Shrī Rāma embraced you with a heart full of joy.

raghupati kīnhī bahuta baṛāī, tuma mama priya bharatahiṁ sama bhāī.

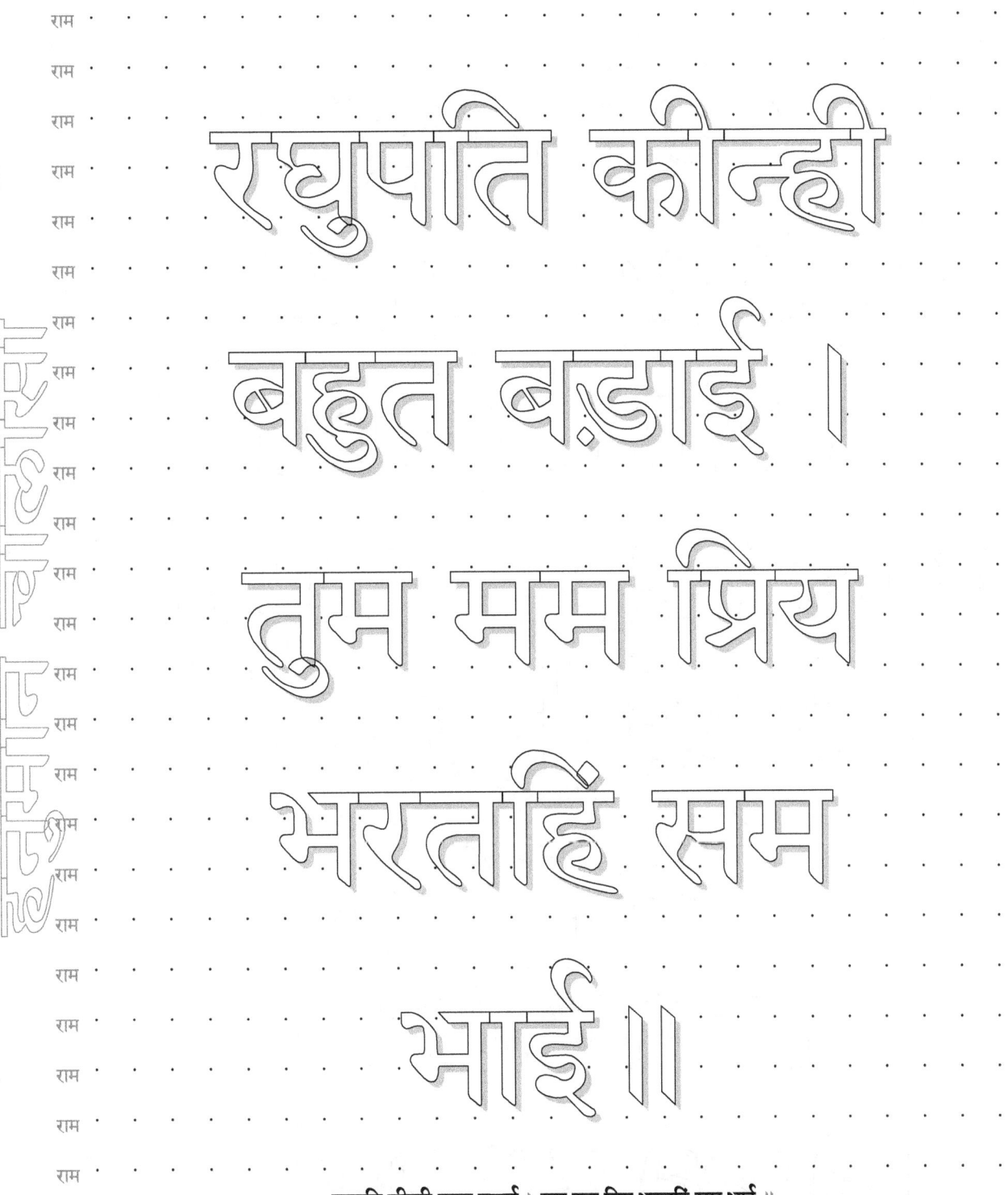

रघुपति कीन्ही बहुत बड़ाई । तुम मम प्रिय भरतहिं सम भाई ॥
raghupati kīnhī bahuta baṛāī, tuma mama priya bharatahiṁ sama bhāī. 12.
Rāma, King of Raghus, extolled you profusely and then He proclaimed: You are to me just like Bharata, dear brother of mine.

sahasa badana tumharo jasa gāvaiṁ, asa kahi śrīpati kaṁṭha lagāvaiṁ .

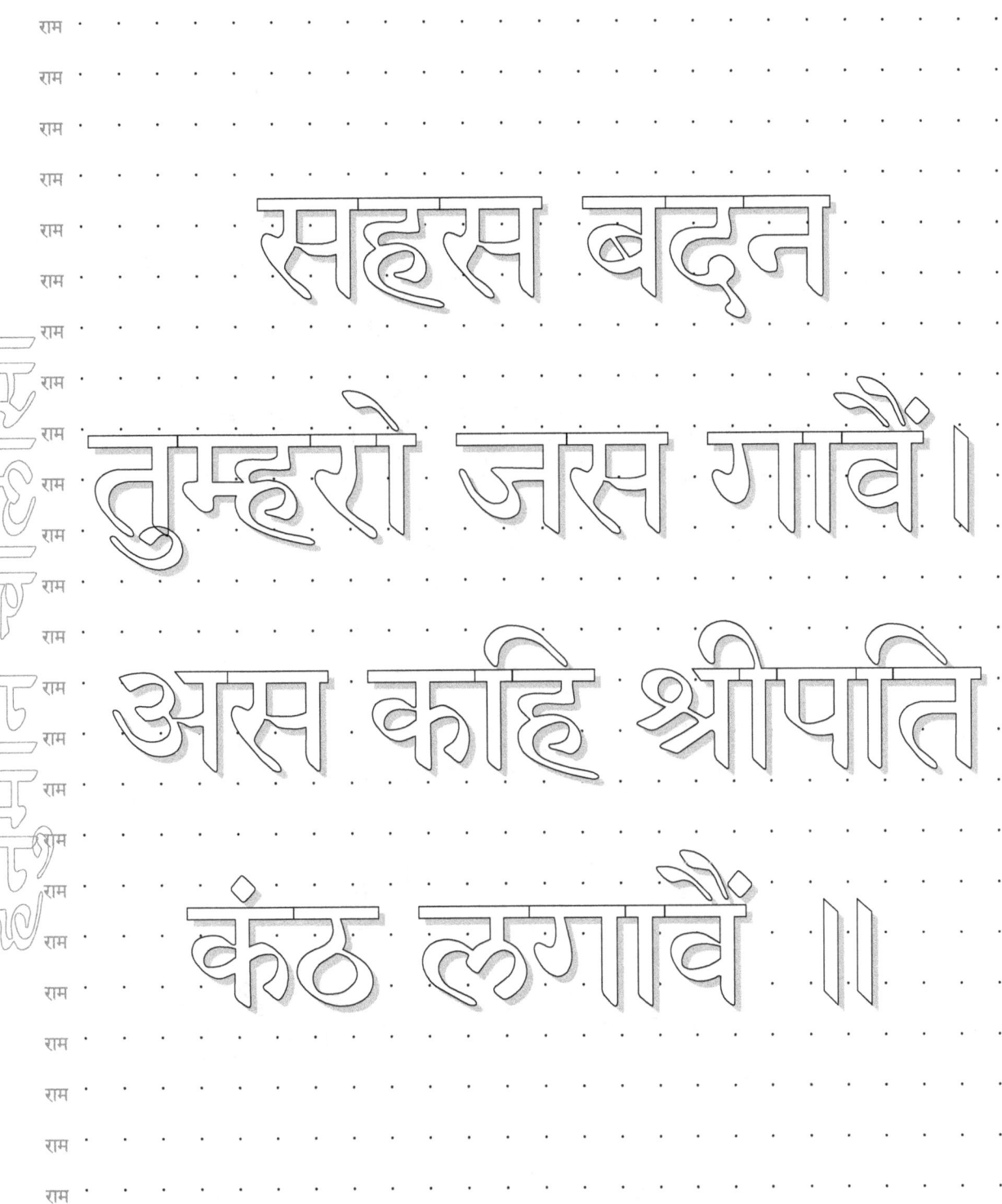

सहस बदन तुम्हरो जस गावैं । अस कहि श्रीपति कंठ लगावैं ॥
sahasa badana tumharo jasa gāvaiṁ, asa kahi śrīpati kaṁṭha lagāvaiṁ. 13.
Thousands of beings are singing your praise—with those words to you, Rāma again to you, unto His heart, did raise.

sanak-ādika brahmādi muniśā , nārada śārada sahita ahiśā.

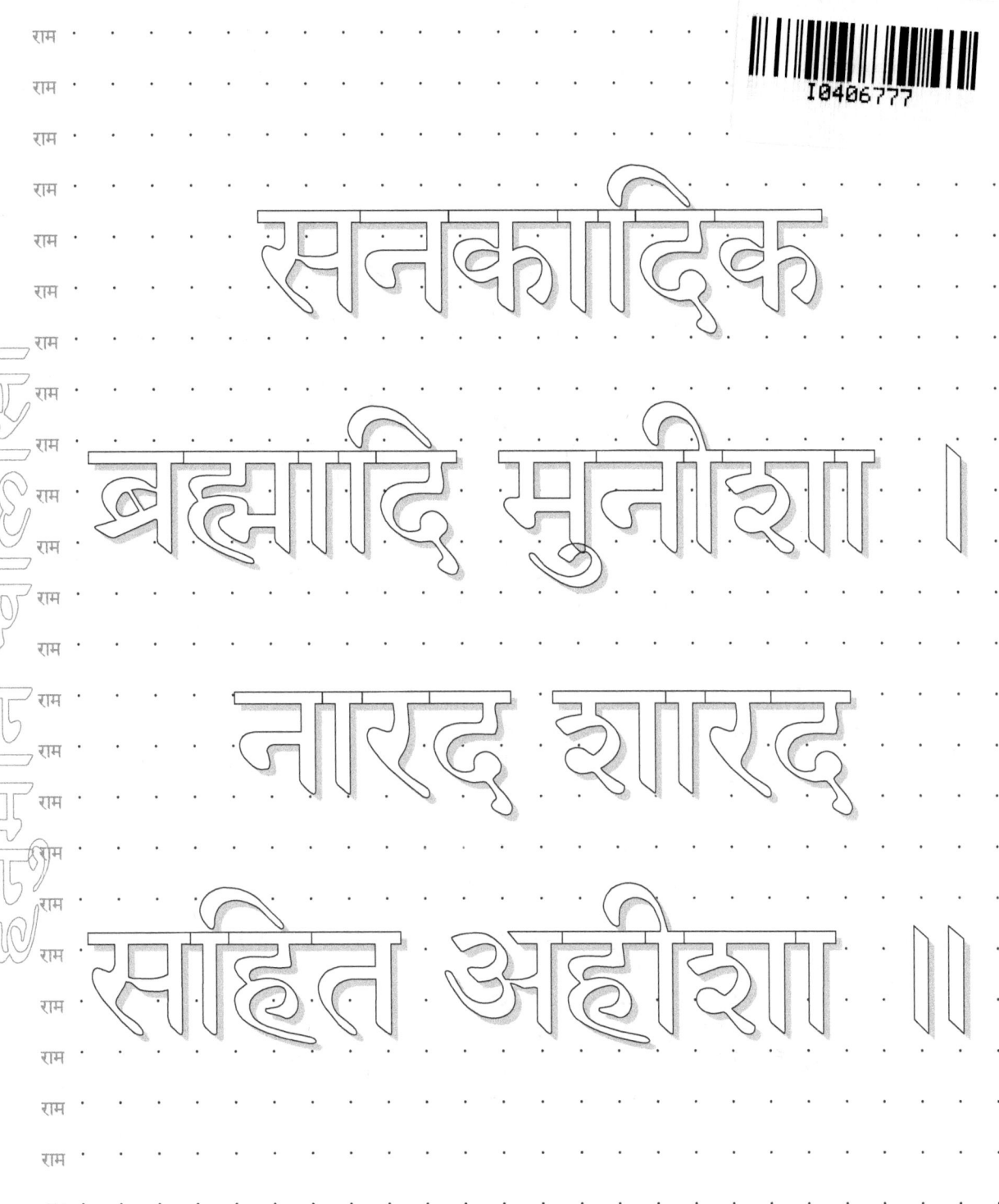

सनकादिक ब्रह्मादि मुनीशा । नारद शारद सहित अहीशा ॥
sanak-ādika brahmādi munīśā, nārada śārada sahita ahīśā. 14.
Celibate *Rishis* like Sanaka; gods like Brahmmā; the foremost *Munis*; Nārad, Saraswatī with Shiva and Vishnu;

jama kubera digapāla jahām̐ te,
kabi kobida kahi sakai kahām̐ te.

जम कुबेर दिगपाल जहाँ ते । कबि कोबिद कहि सकै कहाँ ते ॥
jama kubera digapāla jahāṁ te, kabi kobida kahi sakai kahāṁ te. 15.
the eight *Dikpālas* including Yama and Kubera—they all tell you glory but fail to fully delineate it;
how then can mere mortals, poets and Vedic scholars sing your laurels?

tuma upakāra sugrīvahiṁ kīnhā,
rāma milāya rāja pada dīnhā.

तुम उपकार सुग्रीवहिं कीन्हा । राम मिलाय राज पद दीन्हा ॥
tuma upakāra sugrīvahiṁ kīnhā, rāma milāya rāja pada dīnhā. 16.
You bestowed favor upon Sugrīva—you brought him near to Shri Rāma and made him the King of Kishkindhā.

tumharo maṁtra bibhīṣaṇa mānā, laṁkeśvara bhae saba jaga jānā .

तुम्हरो मंत्र विभीषन माना । लंकेश्वर भए सब जग जाना ॥
tumharo maṁtra bibhīṣana mānā, laṁkeśvara bhae saba jaga jānā. 17.
Vibhīshan accepted your Mantra, and as consequence became the King of Shri Lankā—this is well known throughout the world.

juga sahastra jojana para bhānū,
lilyo tāhi madhura phala jānū.

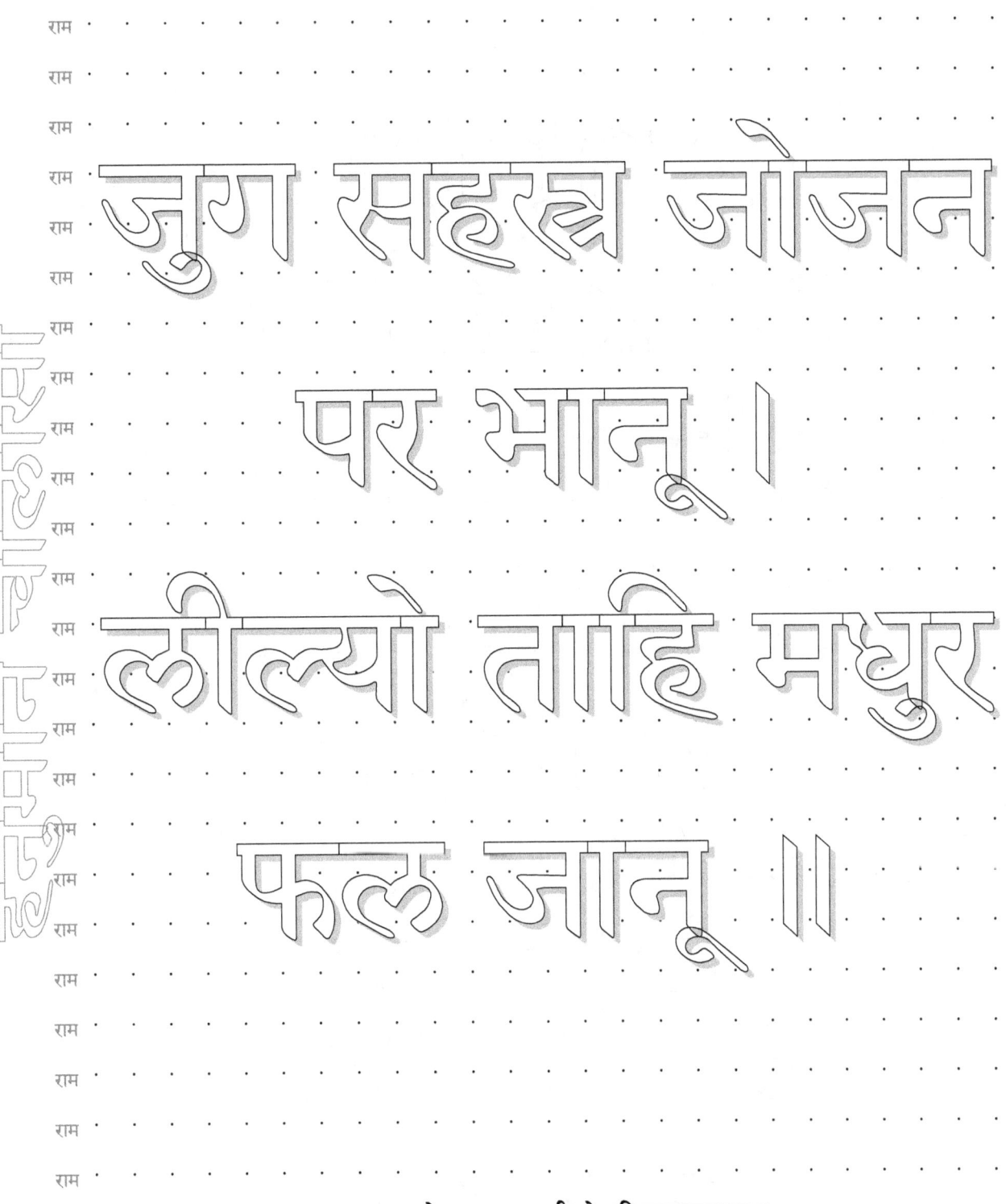

जुग सहस्र जोजन पर भानू । लील्यो ताहि मधुर फल जानू ॥
juga sahastra jojana para bhānū, līlyo tāhi madhura phala jānū. 18.
At a thousand *Yuga Yojan* is the Sun, and mistaking it for a sweet fruit, you supped it up—while you were still an infant.

prabhu mudrikā meli mukha māhīṁ,
jaladhi lāṁghi gaye acaraja nāhīṁ.

प्रभु मुद्रिका मेलि मुख माहीं । जलधि लाँघि गये अचरज नाहीं ॥
prabhu mudrikā meli mukha māhīṁ, jaladhi lāṁghi gaye acaraja nāhīṁ. 19.
The ring of the Lord you placed in your mouth and then leaped across the ocean to give it to Sītā. But what wonder is there in that? [Verily, scaling the impossible comes to you with ease.]

durgama kāja jagata ke jete, sugama anugraha tumhare tete.

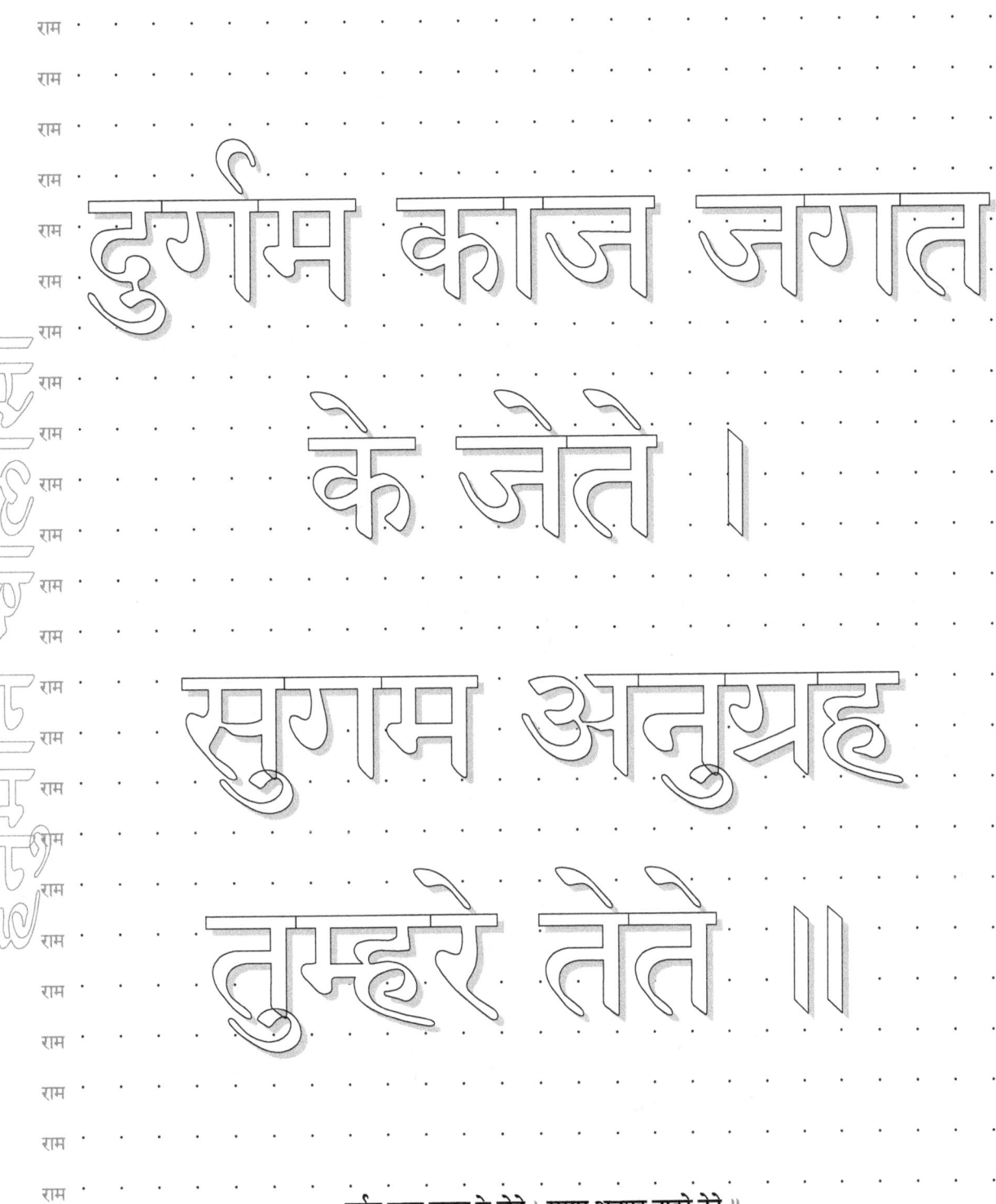

दुर्गम काज जगत के जेते । सुगम अनुग्रह तुम्हरे तेते ॥
durgama kāja jagata ke jete, sugama anugraha tumhare tete. 20.
All the difficult tasks of the world become easy were it your pleasure—if there, O Lord, be the favor of your grace.

rāma duāre tuma rakhavāre, hota na ājñā binu paisāre.

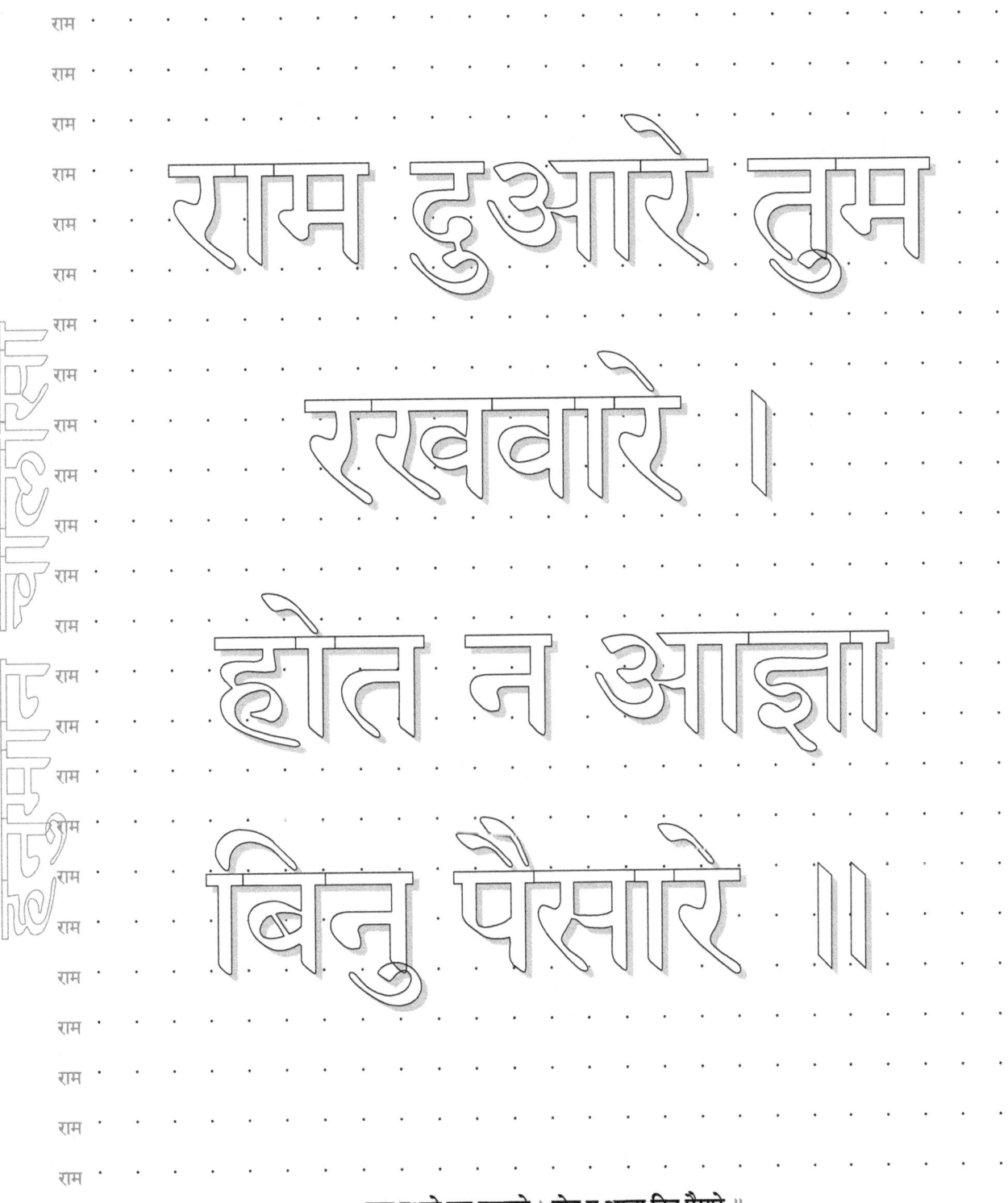

राम दुआरे तुम रखवारे । होत न आज्ञा बिनु पैसारे ॥
rāma duāre tuma rakhavāre, hota na ājñā binu paisāre. 21.
You are the keeper and protector of the gateway to Rāma; without your bidding, nobody can enter the abode of Shrī Rāma.

saba sukha lahaiṁ tumhārī śaranā, tuma rakṣaka kāhū ko ḍara nā .

सब सुख लहैं तुम्हारी शरना । तुम रक्षक काहू को डर ना ॥
saba sukha lahaiṁ tumhārī śaranā, tuma rakṣaka kāhū ko ḍara nā. 22.
Every happiness abides with those who bide under your protection. With you as one's guardian, there is never a cause of any fear.

āpana teja samhāro āpai,
tīnaum loka hāṁka te kāṁpai.

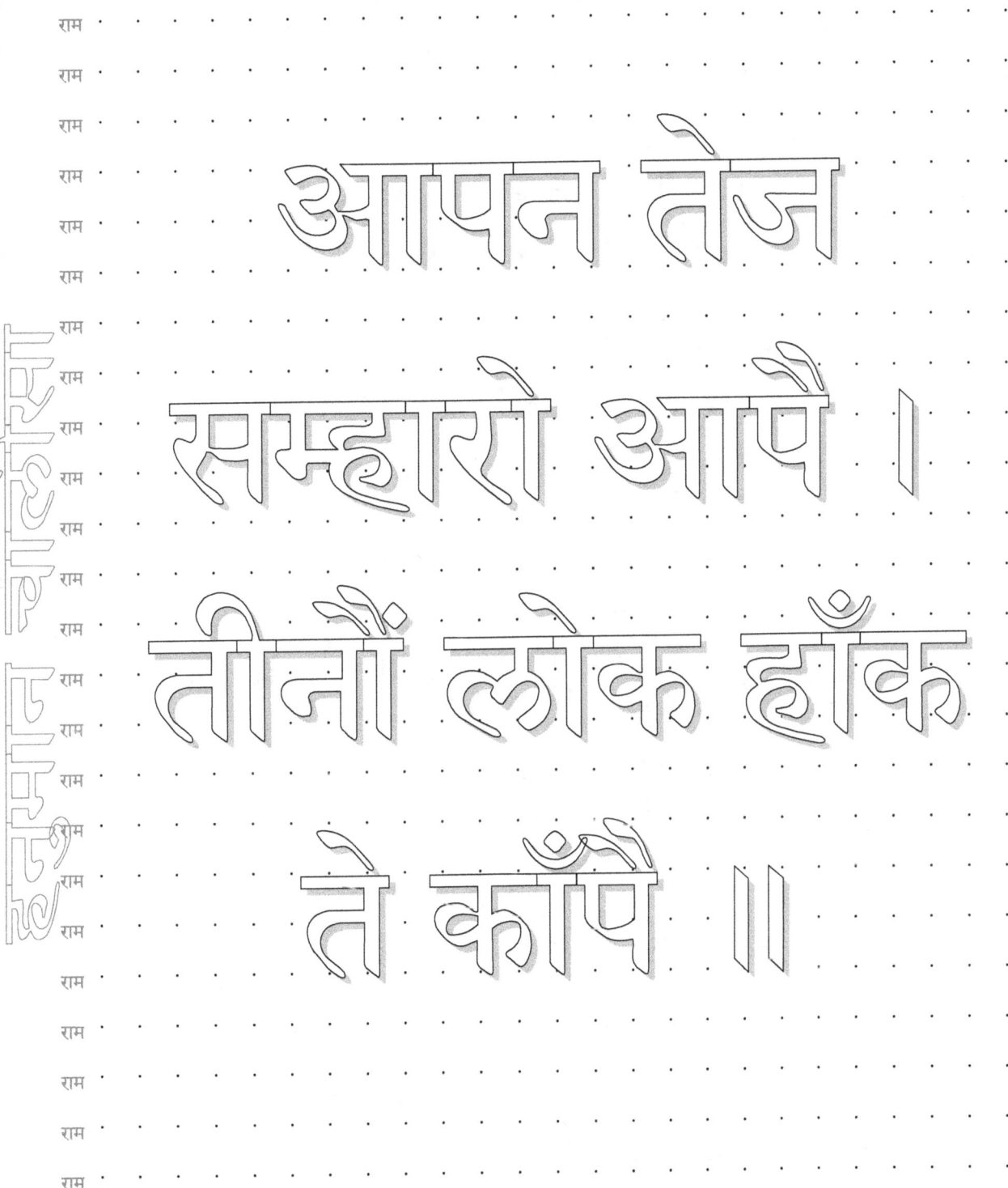

आपन तेज सम्हारो आपै । तीनौं लोक हाँक ते काँपै ॥
āpana teja samhāro āpai, tīnauṁ loka hāṁka te kāṁpai. 23.
You alone can withstand your own splendor; verily the three worlds quake when your thunder.

bhūta piśāca nikaṭa nahiṁ āvai,
mahābīra jaba nāma sunāvai.

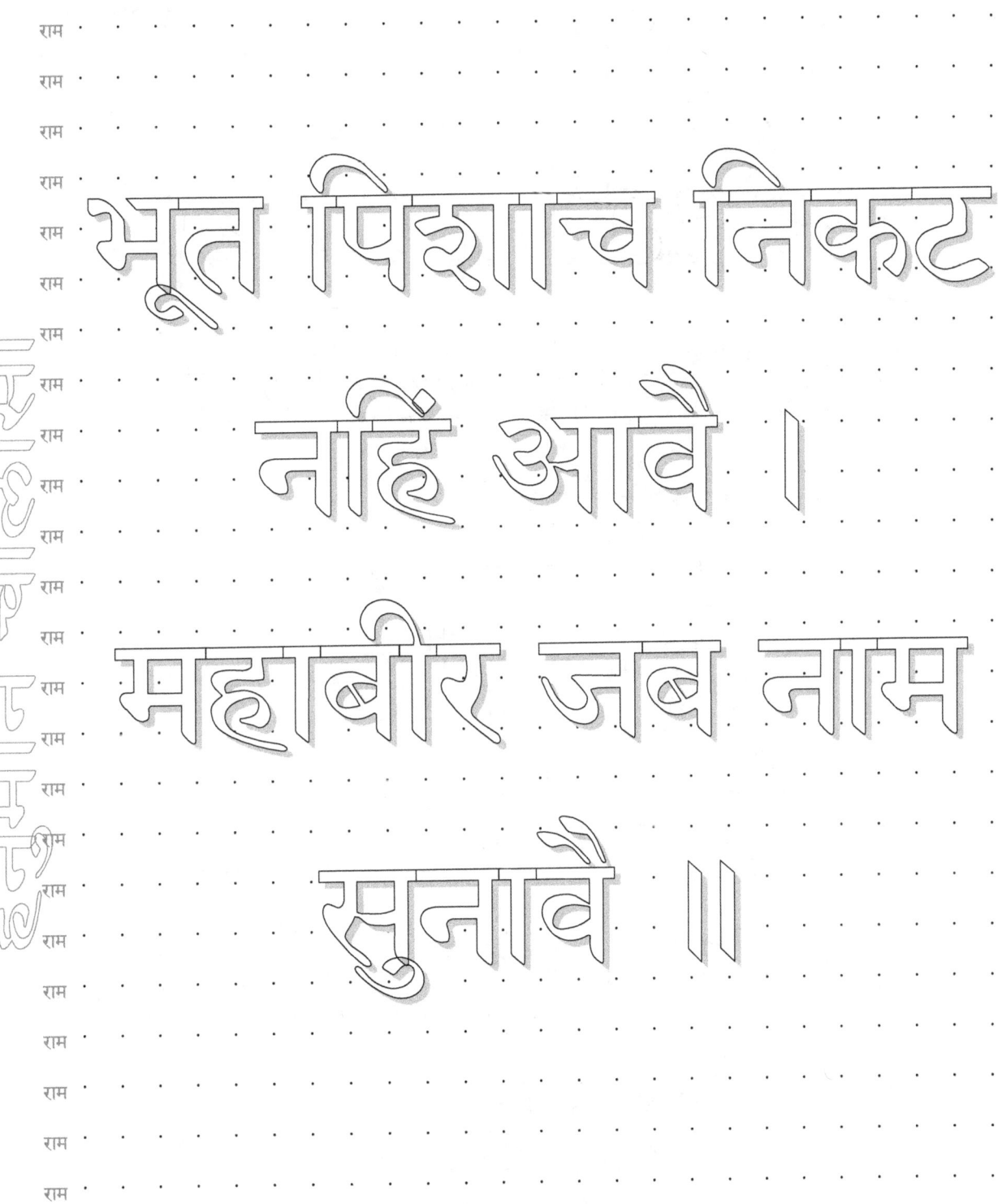

भूत पिशाच निकट नहिं आवै । महाबीर जब नाम सुनावै ॥
bhūta piśāca nikaṭa nahiṁ āvai, mahābīra jaba nāma sunāvai. 24.
Evil spirits and ghosts dare come near not—when the chant of Mahābira, your name, is invoked.

nāsai roga harai saba pīrā, japata niramtara hanumata bīrā.

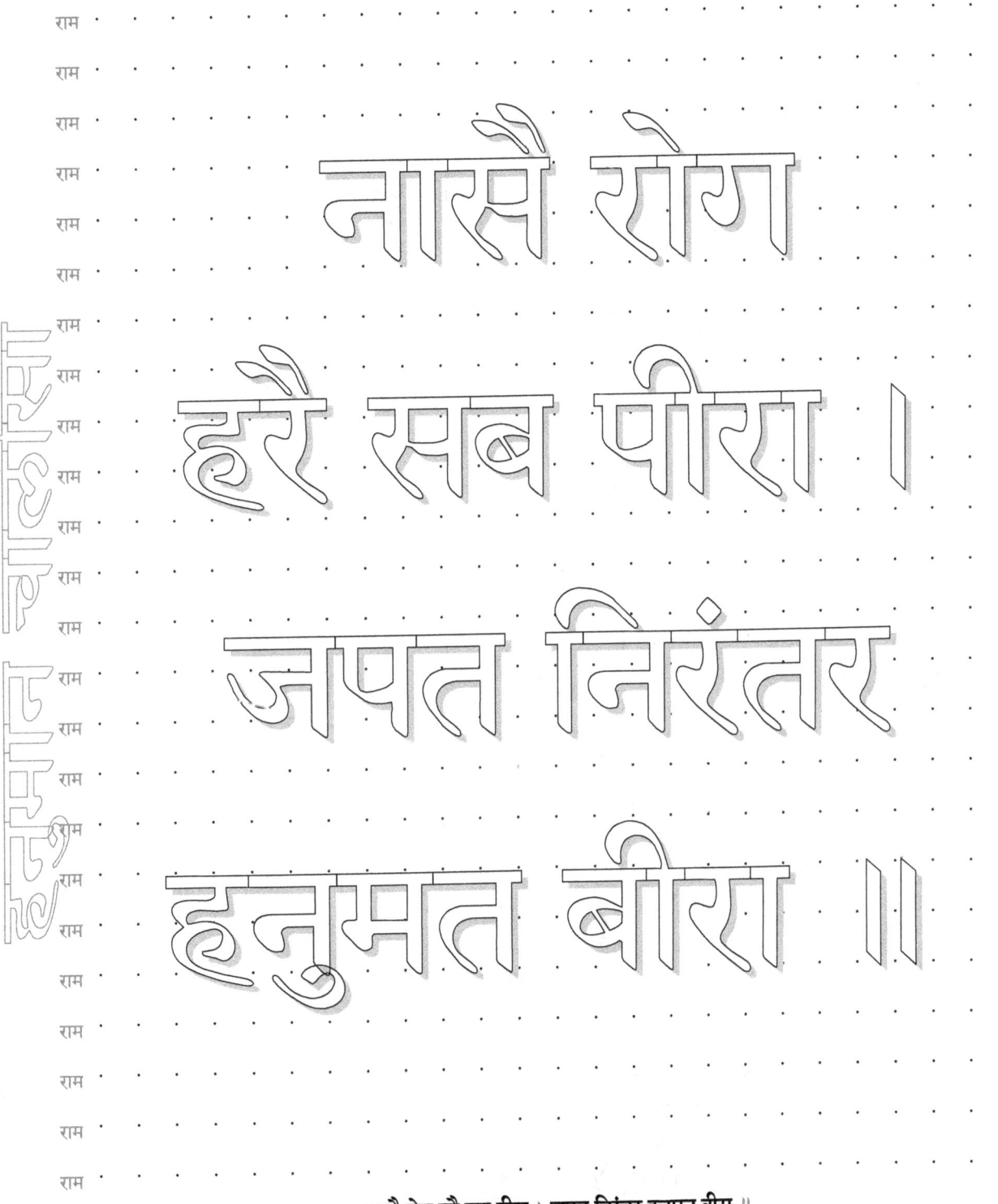

नासै रोग हरै सब पीरा । जपत निरंतर हनुमत बीरा ॥
nāsai roga harai saba pīrā, japata niraṁtara hanumata bīrā. 25.
All diseases are destroyed, all pains are ended—with the constant chant of the Name 'Hanumān', the Mighty-Brave-Supreme.

saṁkaṭa te hanumāna churāvai, mana krama bacana dhyāna jo lāvai.

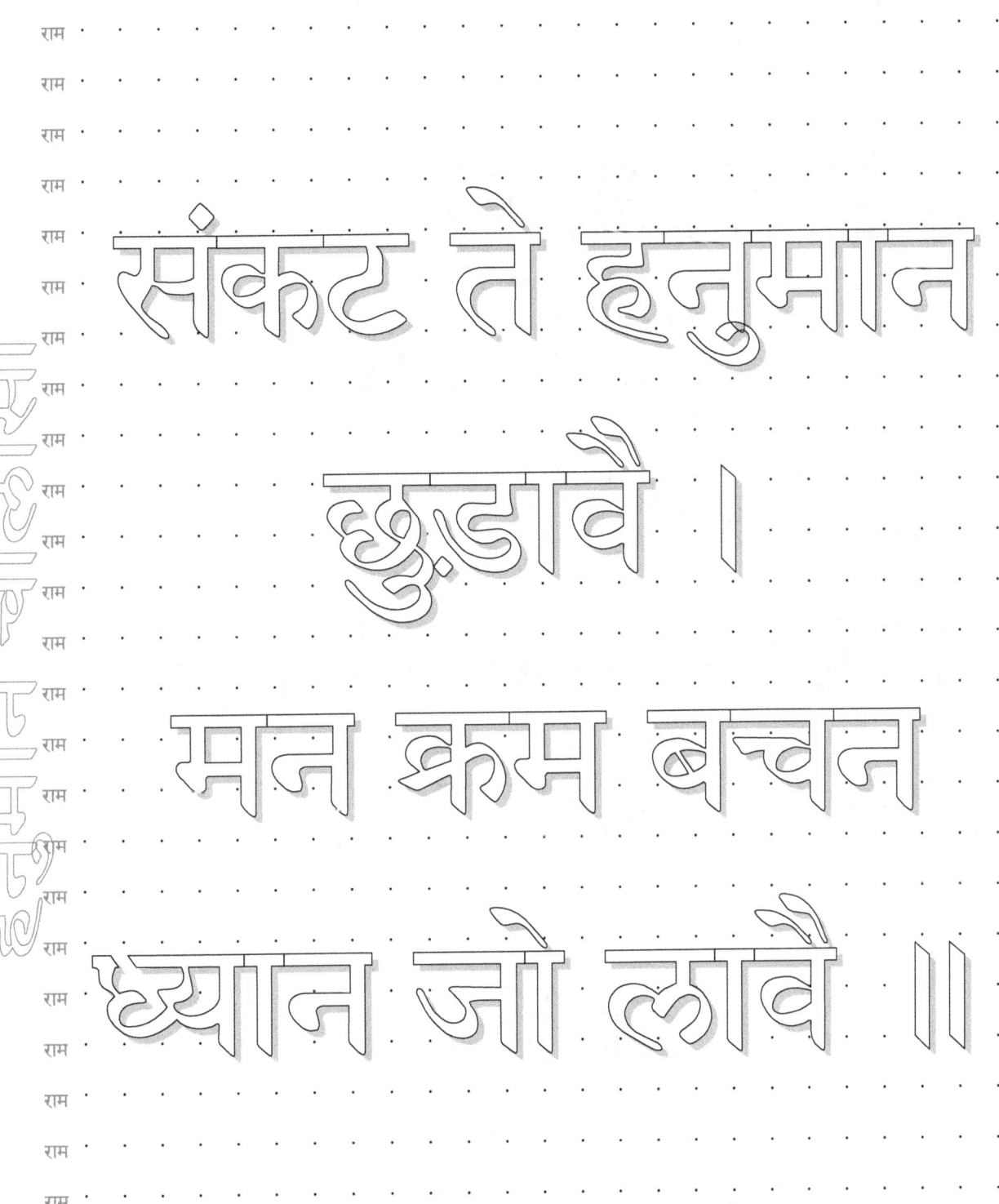

संकट ते हनुमान छुड़ावै । मन क्रम बचन ध्यान जो लावै ॥
saṁkaṭa te hanumāna chuṛāvai, mana krama bacana dhyāna jo lāvai. 26.
Lord Hanumān removes all afflictions, all adversities—for those who dwell on Hanumān through their heart, words and deeds.

saba para rāma tapasvī rājā, tina ke kāja sakala tuma sājā.

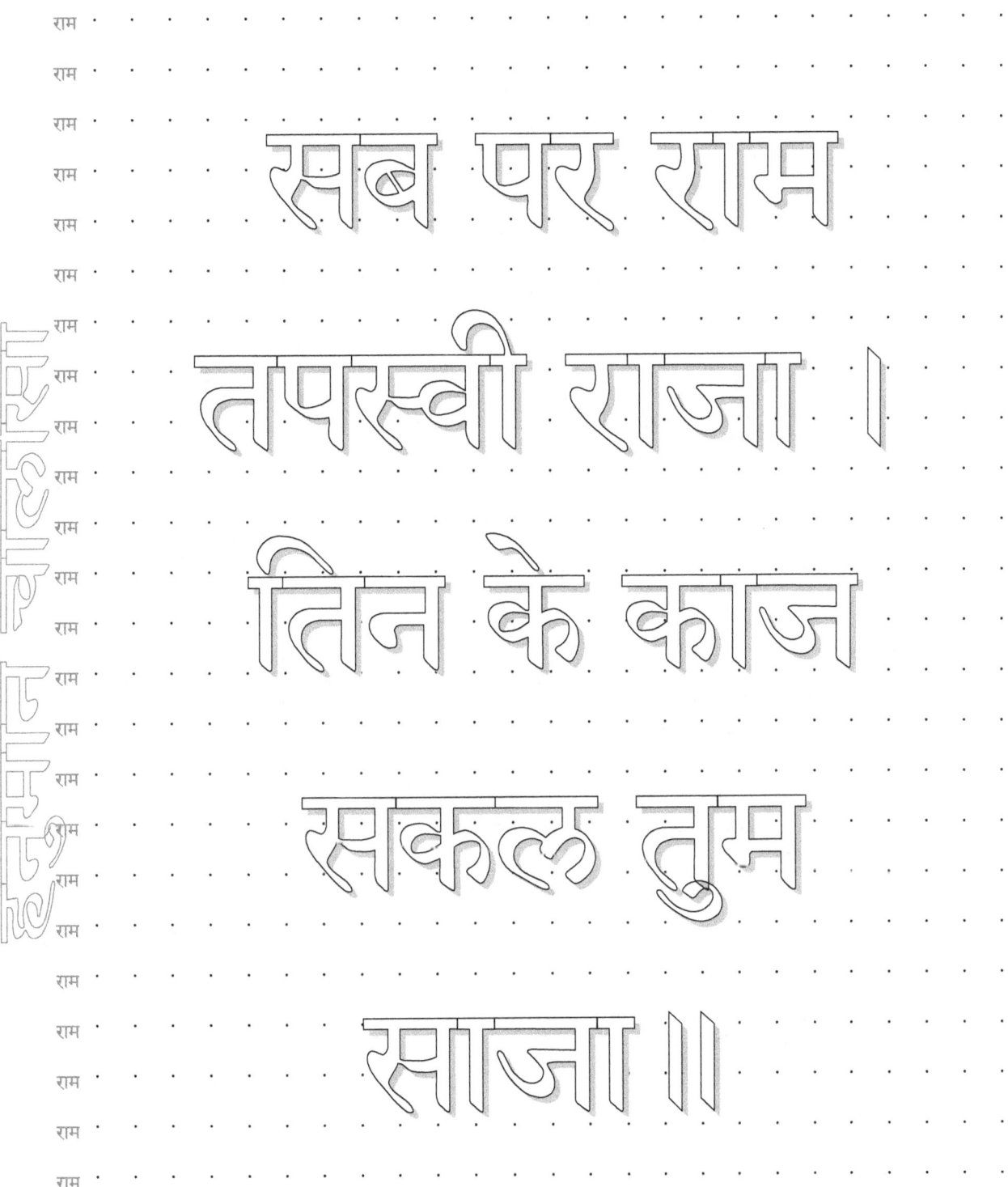

सब पर राम तपस्वी राजा । तिन के काज सकल तुम साजा ॥
saba para rāma tapasvī rājā, tina ke kāja sakala tuma sājā. 27.
Rāma, the Ascetic-King, is the sovereign ruler over all; and it is you who administer his works.

aura manoratha jo kou lāvai, tāsu amita jīvana phala pāvai.

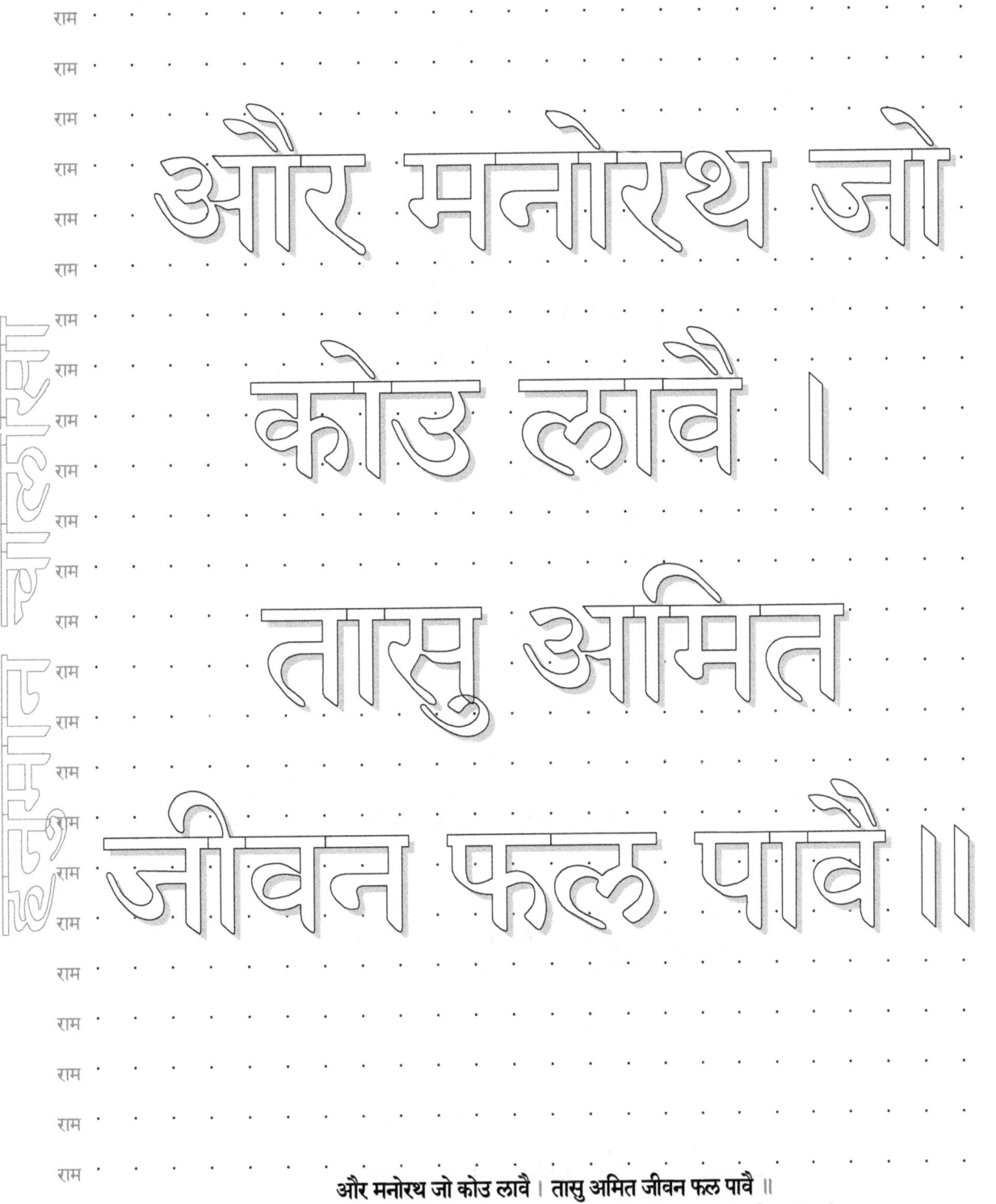

और मनोरथ जो कोउ लावै । तासु अमित जीवन फल पावै ॥
aura manoratha jo kou lāvai, tāsu amita jīvana phala pāvai. 28.
When one comes before you with a heart's desire, you yield unto him unremitting fruits—for the whole life in entire.

cāroṁ juga paratāpa tumhārā, hai parasiddha jagata ujiyārā.

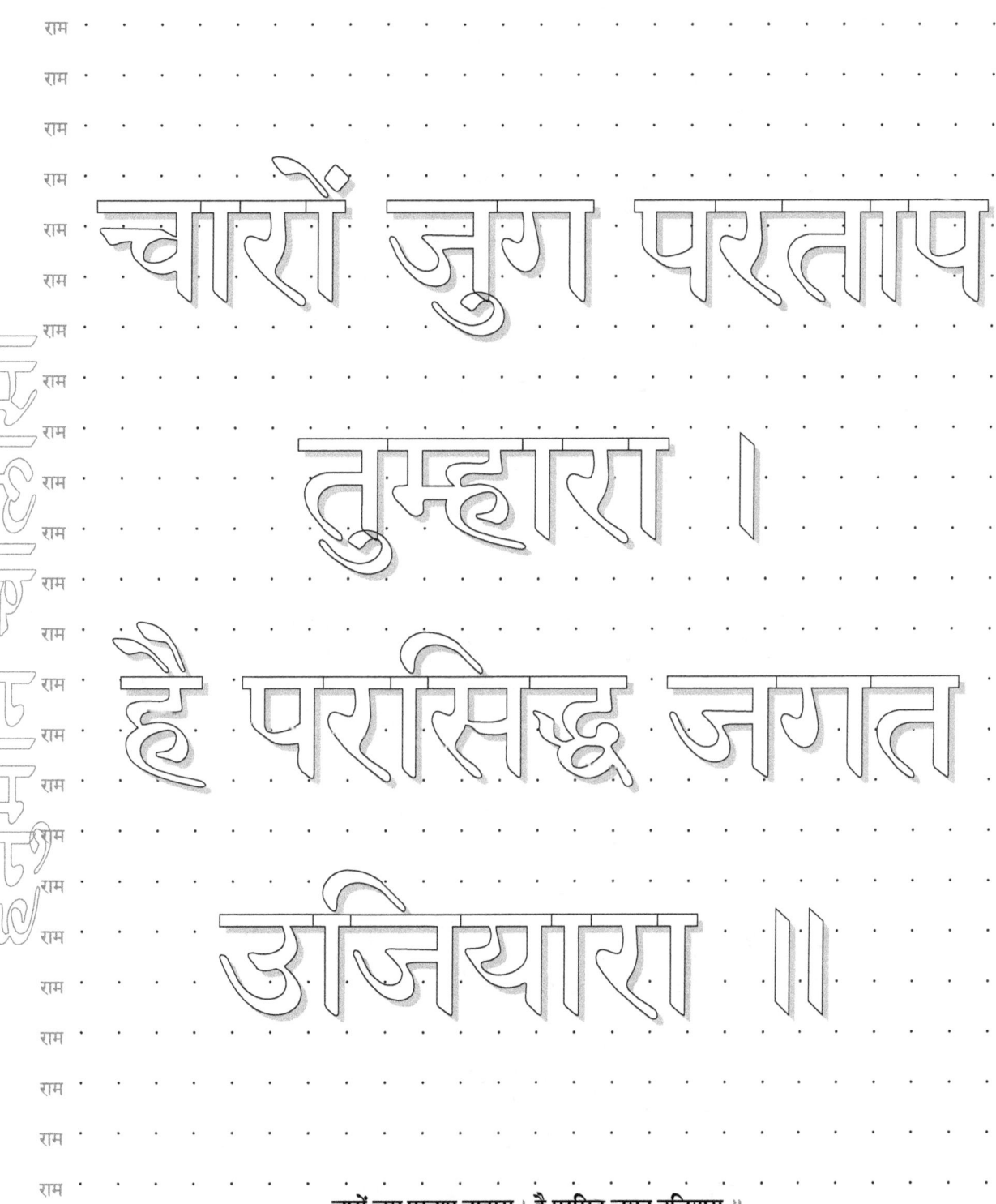

चारों जुग परताप तुम्हारा । है परसिद्ध जगत उजियारा ॥
cāroṁ juga paratāpa tumhārā, hai parasiddha jagata ujiyārā. 29.
Your resplendency persists across all Times; in all the four *Yugas*, your fame illumines throughout the universe.

sādhu saṁta ke tuma rakhavāre, asura nikaṁdana rāma dulāre.

साधु संत के तुम रखवारे । असुर निकंदन राम दुलारे ॥
sādhu saṁta ke tuma rakhavāre, asura nikaṁdana rāma dulāre. 30.
You—dear-most (son) of Rāma—are the guardian of the saintly, virtuous, wise; and you are the destroyer of the fiends and the vile.

aṣṭa siddhi nava nidhi ke dātā,
asa bara dīnha jānakī mātā.

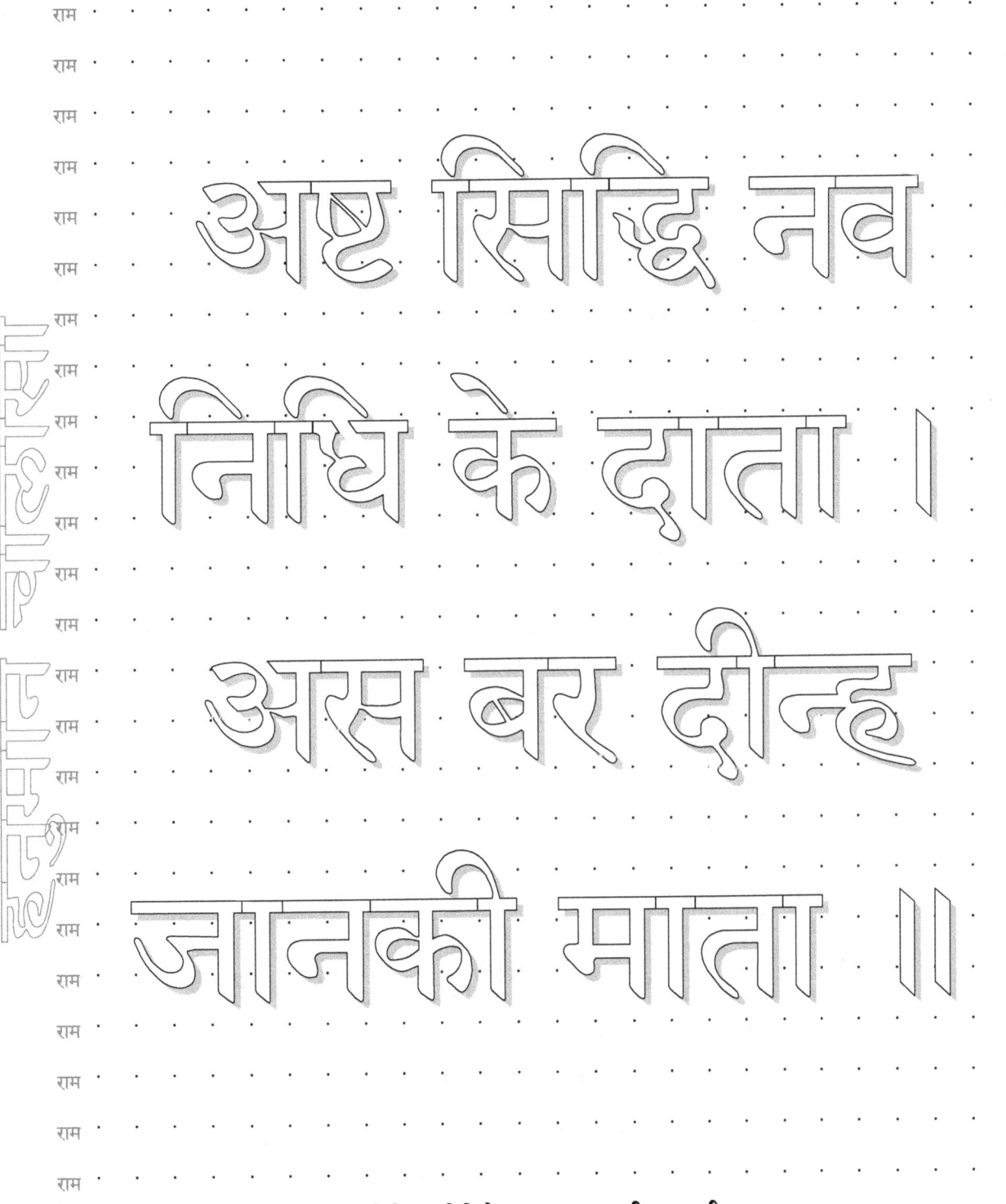

अष्ट सिद्धि नव निधि के दाता । अस बर दीन्ह जानकी माता ॥
aṣṭa siddhi nava nidhi ke dātā, asa bara dīnha jānakī mātā. 31.
You are the bestower of all eight *Siddhis* and nine *Nidhis*—Mother Sītā, daughter of Janak, herself endowed you with that power.

rāma rasāyana tumhare pāsā, sadā rahau raghupati ke dāsā .

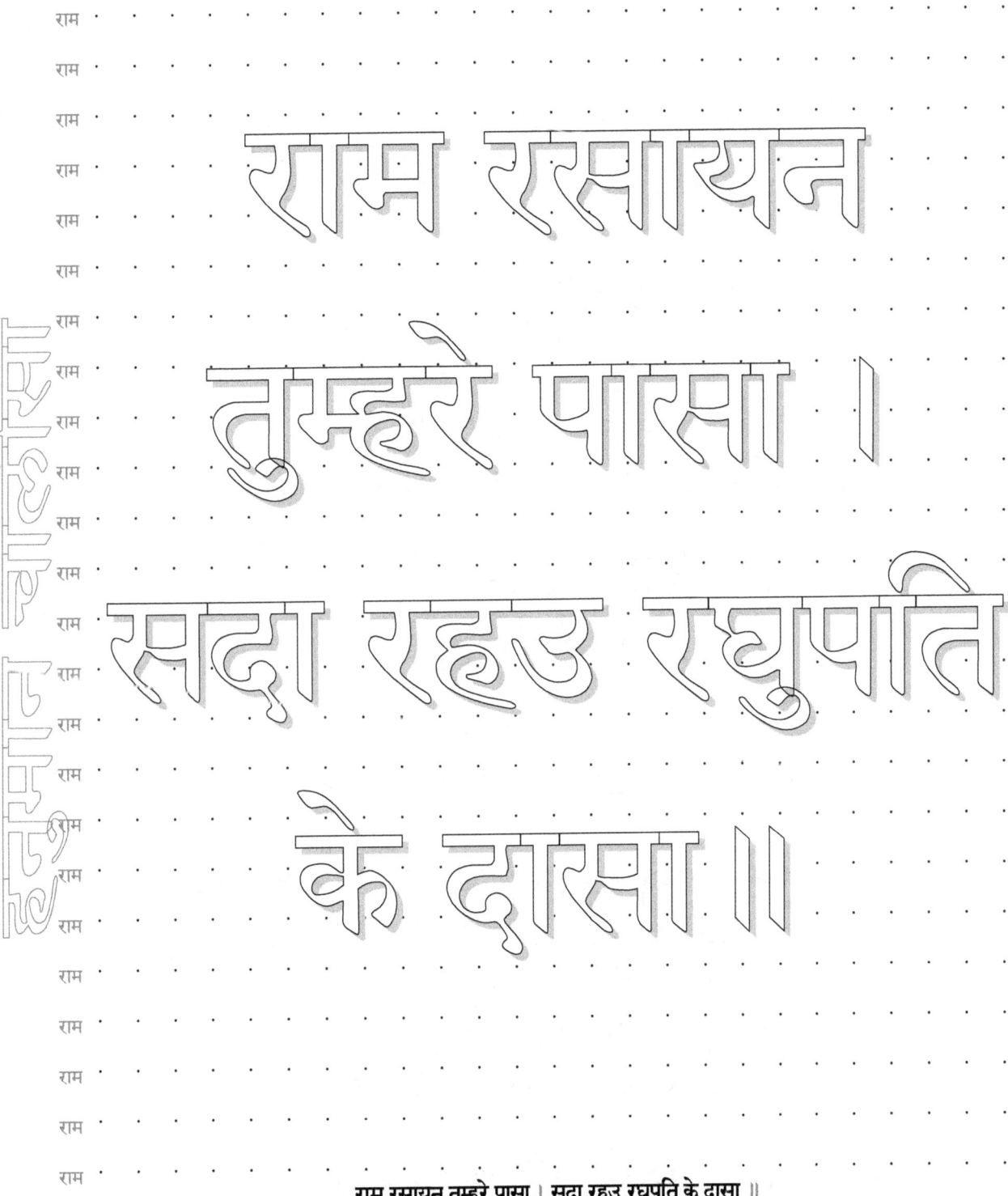

राम रसायन तुम्हरे पासा । सदा रहउ रघुपति के दासा ॥
rāma rasāyana tumhare pāsā, sadā rahau raghupati ke dāsā. 32.
You own the sweet treasure of devotion towards Shri Rāma; you ever abide as the foremost attendant of that Jewel of Raghu scion.

tumhare bhajana rāma ko pāvai, janama janama ke dukha bisarāvai.

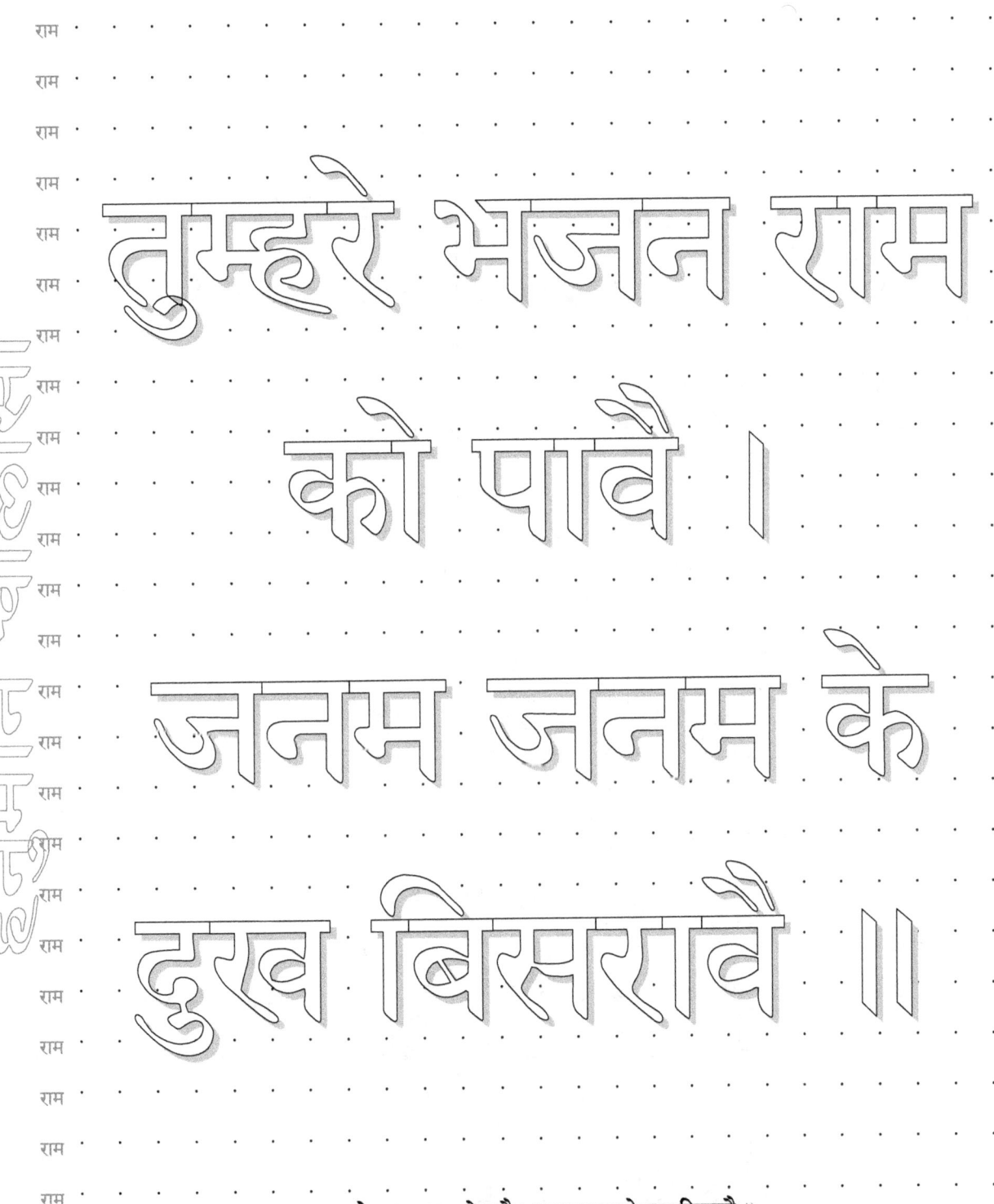

तुम्हरे भजन राम को पावै । जनम जनम के दुख बिसरावै ॥
tumhare bhajana rāma ko pāvai, janama janama ke dukha bisarāvai. 33.
Through devotion to you, one is able to obtain to the Lord; and the adversities and afflictions of millions of births become defeated thereupon;

aṁta kāla raghubara pura jāī, jahāṁ janma haribhakta kahāī.

अंत काल रघुबर पुर जाई । जहाँ जन्म हरिभक्त कहाई ॥
aṁta kāla raghubara pura jāī, jahām̐ janma haribhakta kahāī. 34.
and at the time of their end, one goes to Rāma's own abode—remaining there eternally as Rāma's very own.

aura devatā citta na dharaī, hanumata sei sarba sukha karaī.

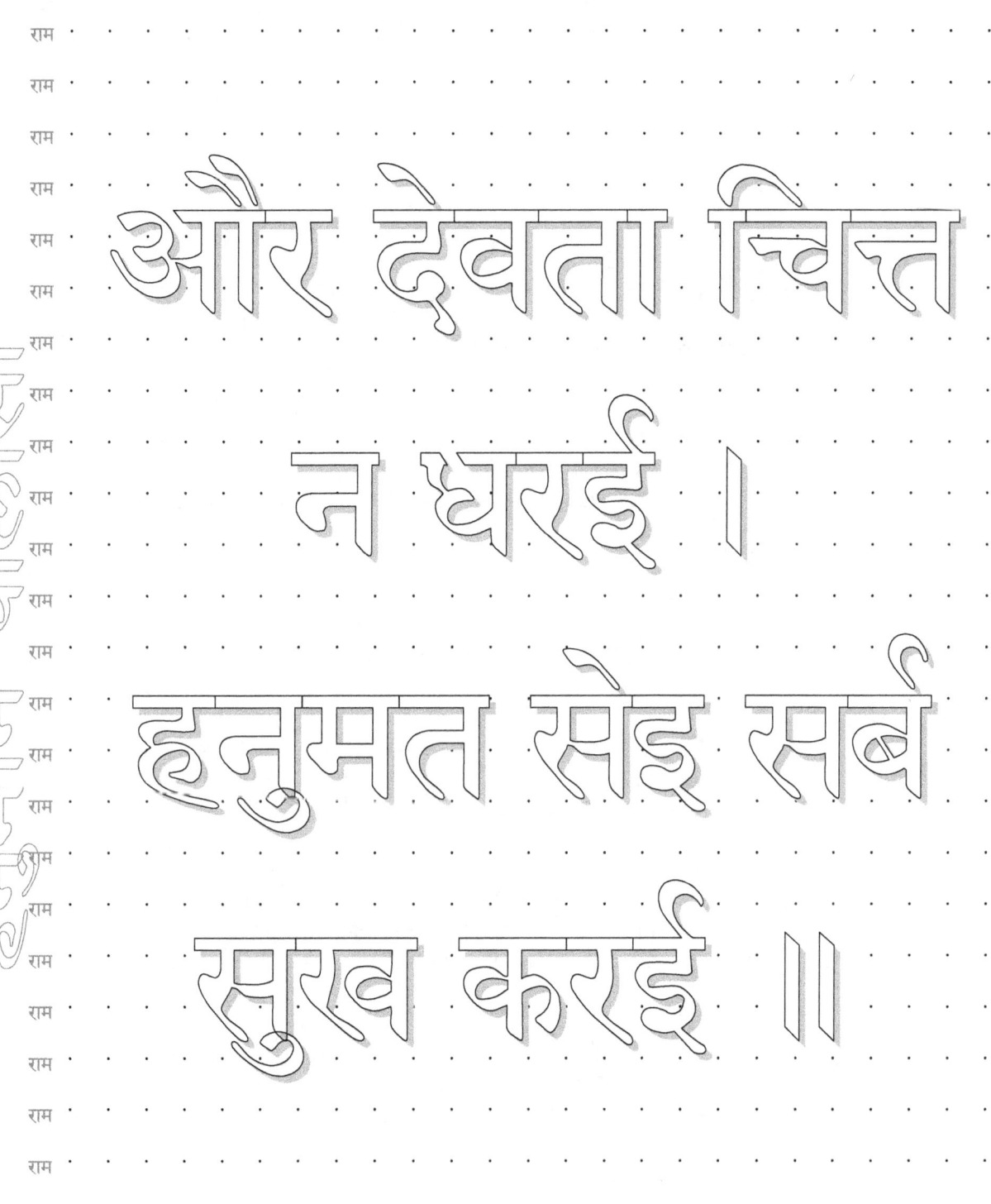

और देवता चित्त न धरई । हनुमत सेइ सर्ब सुख करई ॥
aura devatā citta na dharaī, hanumata sei sarba sukha karaī. 35.
Swearing by no other god and just serving Shrī Hanumān alone—one obtains every felicity in this world and the next.

saṁkaṭa kaṭai miṭai saba pīrā,
jo sumirai hanumata balabīrā.

संकट कटै मिटै सब पीरा । जो सुमिरै हनुमत बलबीरा ॥
saṁkaṭa kaṭai miṭai saba pīrā, jo sumirai hanumata balabīrā. 36.
All troubles are cut short, all pains removed—for those who meditate upon Shri Hanumān, the mighty, brave, supreme.

jaya jaya jaya jaya hanumāna gosāīṁ kṛpā karahu guru deva kī nāīṁ .

जय जय जय हनुमान गोसाईं । कृपा करहु गुरु देव की नाईं ॥
jaya jaya jaya hanumāna gosāīṁ, kṛpā karahu guru deva kī nāīṁ. 37.
Victory to you O Hanumān, O master of senses. May you remain ever victorious, ever triumphant. And do please shower your grace upon us—as lovingly as a Guru does.

yaha śata bāra pāṭha kara joī, chūṭai bamdi mahā sukha soī.

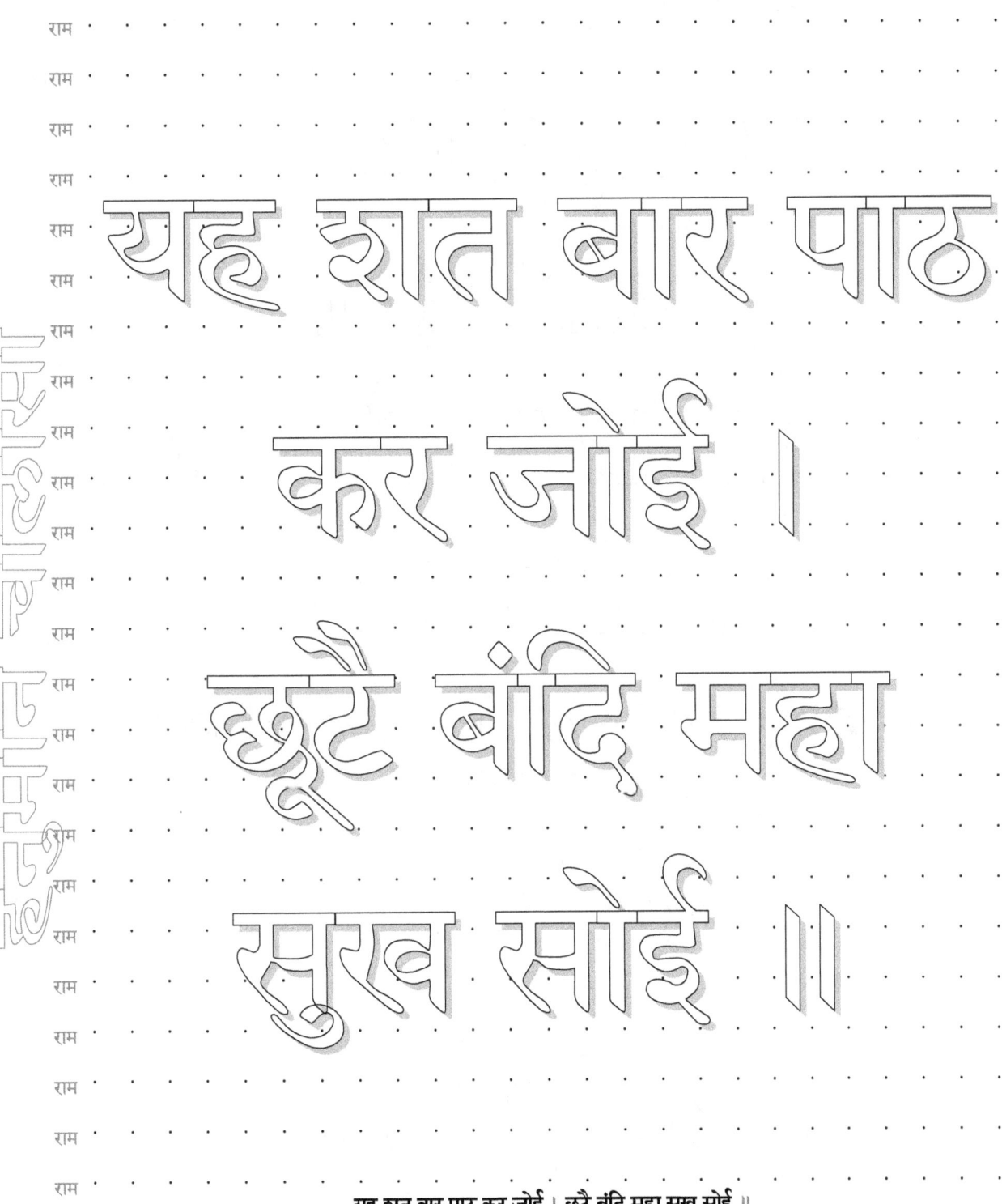

यह शत बार पाठ कर जोई । छूटै बंदि महा सुख सोई ॥
yaha śata bāra pāṭha kara joī, chūṭai baṁdi mahā sukha soī. 38.
One who recites this Hanumān Chālīsā a hundred times is released from all bondages and obtains bliss everlasting.

jo yaha paṛhai hanumāna cālīsā, hoya siddhi sākhī gaurīsā.

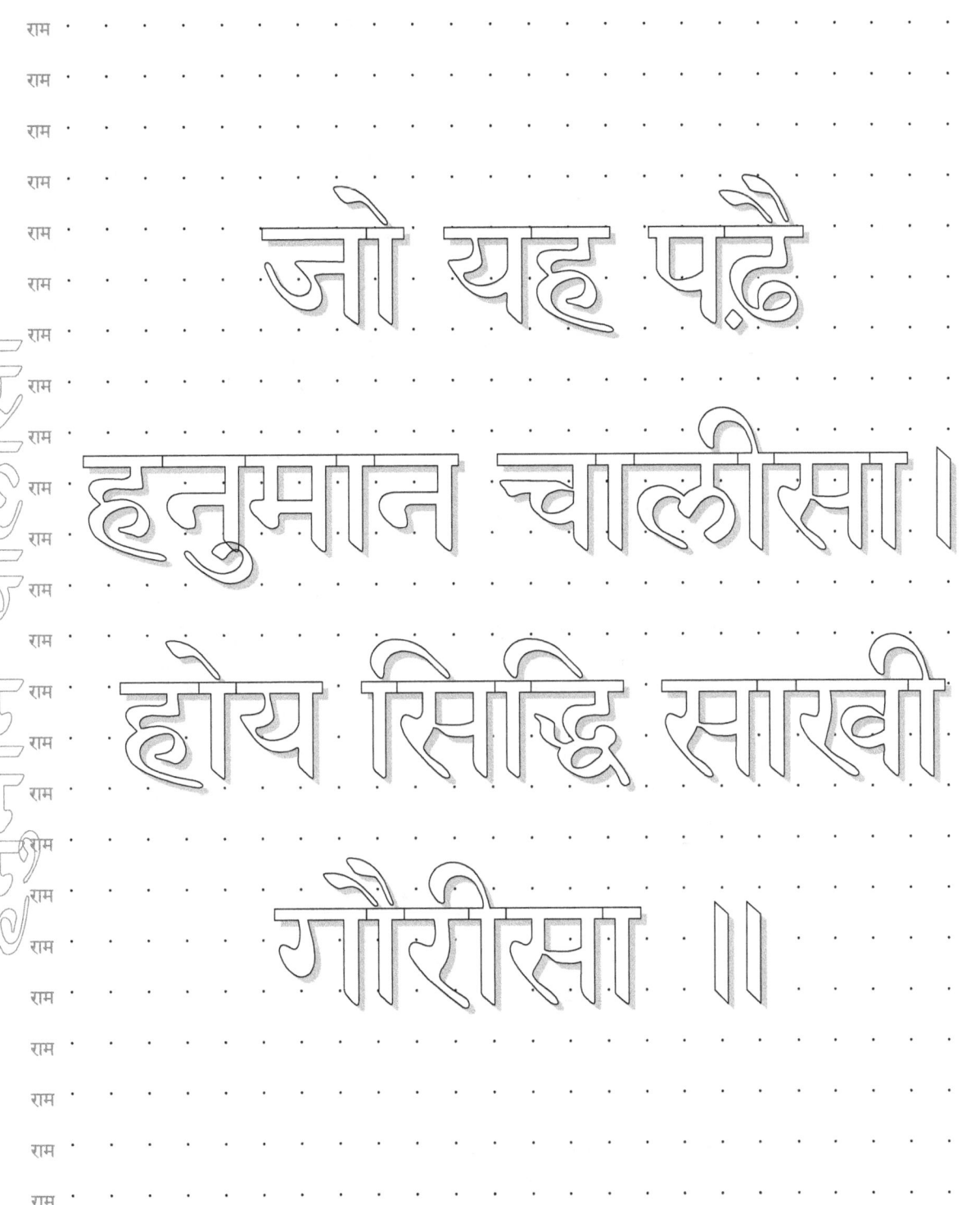

जो यह पढ़ै हनुमान चालीसा । होय सिद्धि साखी गौरीसा ॥
jo yaha paṛhai hanumāna cālīsā, hoya siddhi sākhī gaurīsā. 39.
One who reads this Hanumān Chālīsā becomes a *Siddha*—Gaurī's Lord Shiva himself bears witness to that.

tulasīdāsa sadā hari cerā, kījai nātha hṛdaya mahaṁ ḍerā.

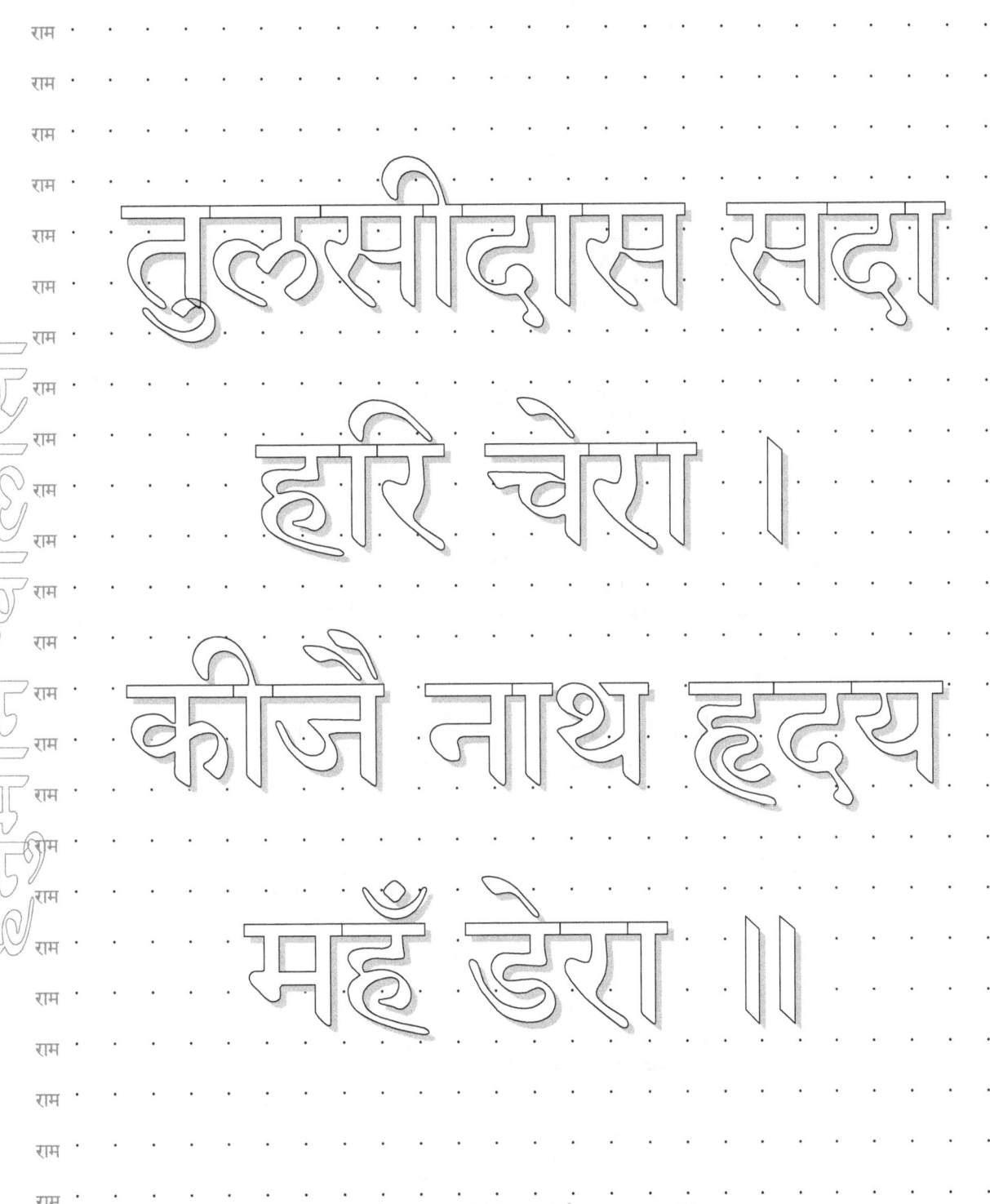

तुलसीदास सदा हरि चेरा । कीजै नाथ हृदय महँ डेरा ॥
tulasī-dāsa sadā hari cerā, kījai nātha hṛdaya mahaṁ ḍerā. 40.
Tulsīdās is ever a humble disciple of Shrī Rāma; O Lord Hanumān, do please take up thy abode in my heart as well (since Rāma is already there).

(dohā)

pavana tanaya samkaṭa harana mamgala mūrati rūpa,

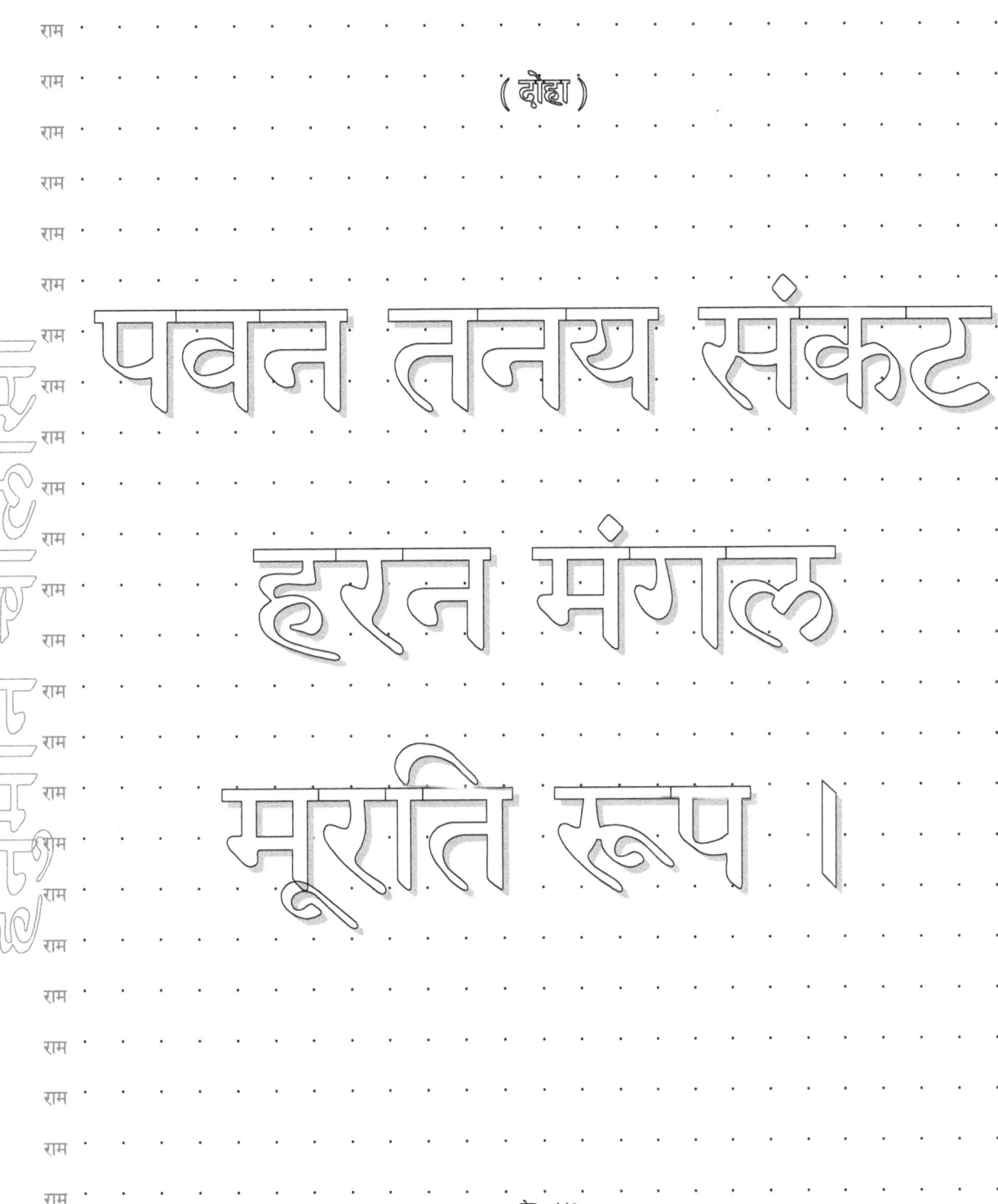

दोहा - dohā
पवन तनय संकट हरन मंगल मूरति रूप।
pavana tanaya saṁkaṭa harana maṁgala mūrati rūpa,
O Son-of-Wind—O remover of all disasters and sins—O Radiant-One of the most auspicious visage—

rāma
lakhana sītā
sahita
hṛdaya
basahu sura
bhūpa.

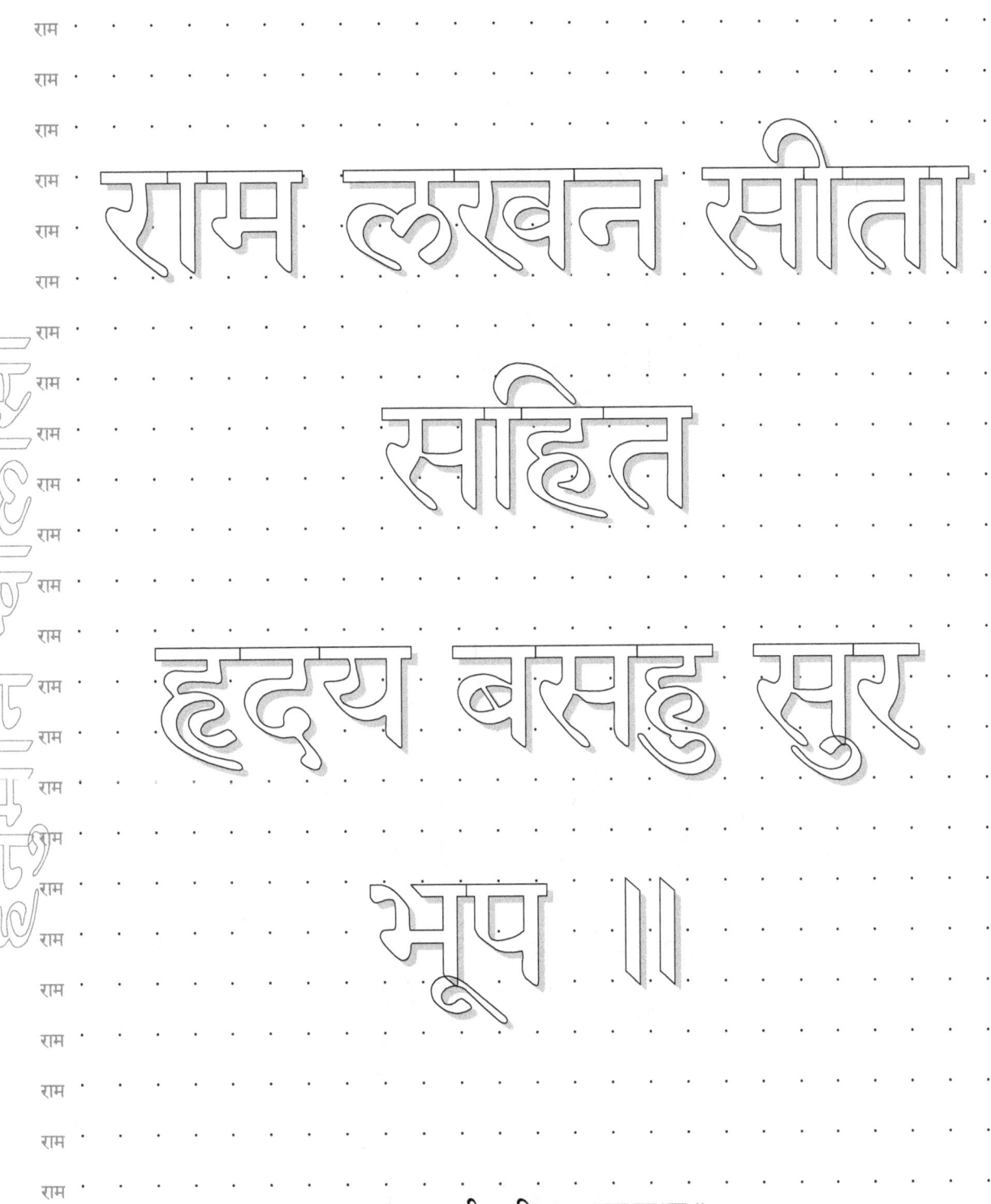

राम लखन सीता सहित हृदय बसहु सुर भूप ॥
rāma lakhana sītā sahita hṛdaya basahu sura bhūpa.
May you ever and ever abide in my heart—along with Sītā, Lakshman, Rāma—O first amongst the gods.

सियावर राम

siyāvara rāma

जय जय
राम

jaya jaya
rāma

मेरे प्रभु

राम

mere

prabhu

rāma

जय जय
राम

jaya jaya
rāma

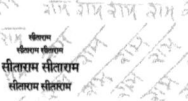

śrījānakīvallabho vijayate

श्री हनुमान चालीसा
śrī-hanumāna-cālīsā

दोहा · dohā

श्रीगुरु चरन सरोज रज निज मन मुकुर सुधारि ।
śrīguru carana saroja raja nija mana mukura sudhāri,
बरनउँ रघुबर बिमल जस जो दायक फल चारि ॥
baranauṁ raghubara bimala jasa jo dāyaka phala cāri.

Cleansing the mirror of my mind with the pollen dust from the lotus feet of the revered Guru, I sing the unsullied glories of Shrī Rāma—the bestower of the four fruits of life.

बुद्धि हीन तनु जानिकै सुमिरौं पवन कुमार ।
buddhi hīna tanu jānikai sumirauṁ pavana kumāra,
बल बुद्धि बिद्या देहु मोहि हरहु कलेश विकार ॥
bala buddhi bidyā dehu mohi harahu kaleśa vikāra.

Knowing this material body to be void of intelligence and seeped in ignorance, I meditate on the Son-of-Wind seeking his favor: Impart to me strength, intelligence, virtuosity; and remove all ailments and imperfections, my Lord.

चौपाई · caupāī

जय हनुमान ज्ञान गुण सागर । जय कपीश तिहुँ लोक उजागर ॥
jaya hanumāna jñāna guṇa sāgara, jaya kapīśa tihuṁ loka ujāgara. 1.

Glory be to Hanumān—the ocean of wisdom and virtues. Victory to the monkey-god whose resplendency irradiates the three spheres of creation.

राम दूत अतुलित बल धामा । अंजनिपुत्र पवनसुत नामा ॥
rāma dūta atulita bala dhāmā, aṁjani-putra pavanasuta nāmā. 2.

Glory be to the divine messenger and servant of Shrī Rāma, the repository of immeasurable strength. Glory be to mother Anjanī's boy, bearing the name Pavana-Suth—Son-of-Wind.

महाबीर बिक्रम बजरंगी । कुमति निवार सुमति के संगी ॥

mahābīra bikrama bajaraṁgī, kumati nivāra sumati ke saṁgī. 3.

O supremely valorous hero of wondrous great deeds, with a body that is strong as diamond: evilness of the mind you cure; a companion you are of those with minds good and pure.

कंचन बरन बिराज सुबेषा । कानन कुंडल कुंचित केशा ॥

kaṁcana barana birāja subeṣā, kānana kuṁḍala kuṁcita keśā. 4.

With a complexion that's molten gold, you shine resplendent in your exquisite form—with rings in your ears and lovely curly locks.

हाथ बज्र और ध्वजा बिराजै । काँधे मूँज जनेऊ साजै ॥

hātha bajra aura dhvajā birājai, kāṁdhe mūṁja janeū sājai. 5.

In your hands are held a mace and a flag; and there's *Munji* and *Janeu* embellished across your shoulders, well adorned.

शङ्कर स्वयं केशरीनंदन । तेज प्रताप महा जग बंदन ॥

śaṅkara svayaṁ keśarīnaṁdana, teja pratāpa mahā jaga baṁdana. 6.

You are Shankar himself (embodied as Hanuman), born to the mighty Keshari—the delight of his heart; your majesty and prowess is astounding—venerated throughout the universe.

विद्यावान गुणी अति चातुर । राम काज करिबे को आतुर ॥

vidyā-vāna guṇī ati cātura, rāma kāja karibe ko ātura. 7.

Learned in all the sciences, virtuous, most clever and wise—you are ever so eager to do all of Rama's work.

प्रभु चरित्र सुनिबे को रसिया । राम लखन सीता मन बसिया ॥

prabhu caritra sunibe ko rasiyā, rāma lakhana sītā mana basiyā. 8.

Your greatest delight is in listening to the glories of the Lord, and Rāma-Lakshman-Sītā ever reside in your heart; nay—you ever abide in the hearts of Lakshman-Sītā-Rāma.

सूक्ष्म रूप धरि सियहिं दिखावा । बिकट रूप धरि लंक जरावा ॥

sūkṣma rūpa dhari siyahiṁ dikhāvā, bikaṭa rūpa dhari laṁka jarāvā. 9.

भीम रूप धरि असुर सँहारे । रामचन्द के काज सँवारे ॥

bhīma rūpa dhari asura saṁhāre, rāma-candra ke kāja saṁvāre. 10.

When visiting mother Sītā you showed yourself in tiny diminutive form; then growing to fearsome colossal size you burnt the whole of Laṅkā down; assuming a valorous form you destroyed many demons—thus you ever serve to facilitate the works of the Lord-God Shrī Rāma-Chandra.

लाय संजीवनि लखन जियाये । श्री रघुबीर हरषि उर लाये ॥

lāya saṁjīvani lakhana jiyāye, śrī raghu-bīra haraṣi ura lāye. 11.

You brought the *Sanjīvanī* and brought Lakshman back to life—whereupon Shrī Rāma embraced you with a heart full of joy.

रघुपति कीन्हीं बहुत बड़ाई । तुम मम प्रिय भरतहिं सम भाई ॥

raghupati kīnhī bahuta baṛāī, tuma mama priya bharatahiṁ sama bhāī. 12.

Rāma, King of Raghus, extolled you profusely and then He proclaimed: You are to me just like Bharata, dear brother of mine.

सहस बदन तुम्हरो जस गावैं । अस कहि श्रीपति कंठ लगावैं ॥

sahasa badana tumharo jasa gāvaiṁ, asa kahi śrīpati kaṁṭha lagāvaiṁ. 13.

Thousands of beings are singing your praise—with those words to you, Rāma again to you, unto His heart, did raise.

सनकादिक ब्रह्मादि मुनीशा । नारद शारद सहित अहीशा ॥

sanak-ādika brahmādi munīśā, nārada śārada sahita ahīśā. 14.

जम कुबेर दिगपाल जहाँ ते । कबि कोबिद कहि सकै कहाँ ते ॥

jama kubera digapāla jahāṁ te, kabi kobida kahi sakai kahāṁ te. 15.

Celibate *Rishis* like Sanaka; gods like Brahmmā; the foremost *Munis*; Nārad, Saraswatī with Shiva and Vishnu; the eight *Dikpālas* including Yama and Kubera—they all tell you glory but fail to fully delineate it; how then can mere mortals, poets and Vedic scholars sing your laurels?

तुम उपकार सुग्रीवहिं कीन्हा । राम मिलाय राज पद दीन्हा ॥

tuma upakāra sugrīvahiṁ kīnhā, rāma milāya rāja pada dīnhā. 16.

You bestowed favor upon Sugrīva—you brought him near to Shrī Rāma and made him the King of Kishkindhā.

तुम्हरो मंत्र बिभीषन माना । लंकेश्वर भए सब जग जाना ॥

tumharo maṁtra bibhīṣana mānā, laṁkeśvara bhae saba jaga jānā. 17.

Vibhīshan accepted your Mantra, and as consequence became the King of Shrī Lankā—this is well known throughout the world.

जुग सहस्र जोजन पर भानू । लील्यो ताहि मधुर फल जानू ॥

* juga sahastra jojana para bhānū, līlyo tāhi madhura phala jānū. 18.

At a thousand *Yuga Yojan* is the Sun, and mistaking it for a sweet fruit, you supped it up—while you were still an infant.

प्रभु मुद्रिका मेलि मुख माहीं । जलधि लाँघि गये अचरज नाहीं ॥

prabhu mudrikā meli mukha māhīṁ, jaladhi lāṁghi gaye acaraja nāhīṁ. 19.

The ring of the Lord you placed in your mouth and then leaped across the ocean to give it to Sītā. But what wonder is there in that? [Verily, scaling the impossible comes to you with ease.]

दुर्गम काज जगत के जेते | सुगम अनुग्रह तुम्हरे तेते ||
durgama kāja jagata ke jete, sugama anugraha tumhare tete. 20.

All the difficult tasks of the world become easy were it your pleasure—if there, O Lord, be the favor of your grace.

राम दुआरे तुम रखवारे | होत न आज्ञा बिनु पैसारे ||
rāma duāre tuma rakhavāre, hota na ājñā binu paisāre. 21.

You are the keeper and protector of the gateway to Rāma; without your command, nobody can enter the abode of Shrī Rāma.

सब सुख लहैं तुम्हारी शरना | तुम रक्षक काहू को डर ना ||
saba sukha lahaim tumhārī śaranā, tuma rakṣaka kāhū ko ḍara nā. 22.

Every happiness abides with those who bide under your protection. With you as one's guardian, there is never a cause of any fear.

आपन तेज सम्हारो आपै | तीनौं लोक हाँक ते काँपै ||
āpana teja samhāro āpai, tīnaum loka hāṁka te kāṁpai. 23.

You alone can withstand your own splendor; verily the three worlds quake when your thunder.

भूत पिशाच निकट नहिं आवै | महाबीर जब नाम सुनावै ||
bhūta piśāca nikaṭa nahim āvai, mahābīra jaba nāma sunāvai. 24.

Evil spirits and ghosts dare come near not—when the chant of Mahābīra, your name, is invoked.

नासै रोग हरै सब पीरा | जपत निरंतर हनुमत बीरा ||
nāsai roga harai saba pīrā, japata niramtara hanumata bīrā. 25.

All diseases are destroyed, all pains are ended—with the constant chant of the Name 'Hanumān', the Mighty-Brave-Supreme.

संकट ते हनुमान छुड़ावै | मन क्रम बचन ध्यान जो लावै ||
samkaṭa te hanumāna chuṛāvai, mana krama bacana dhyāna jo lāvai. 26.

Lord Hanumān removes all afflictions, all adversities—for those who dwell on Hanumān through their heart, words and deeds.

सब पर राम तपस्वी राजा | तिन के काज सकल तुम साजा ||
saba para rāma tapasvī rājā, tina ke kāja sakala tuma sājā. 27.

Rāma, the Ascetic-King, is the sovereign ruler over all; and it is you who administer his works.

और मनोरथ जो कोउ लावै | तासु अमित जीवन फल पावै ||
aura manoratha jo kou lāvai, tāsu amita jīvana phala pāvai. 28.

When one comes before you with a heart's desire, you yield unto him unremitting fruits—for the whole life in entire.

चारों जुग परताप तुम्हारा । है परसिद्ध जगत उजियारा ॥
cāroṁ juga paratāpa tumhārā, hai parasiddha jagata ujiyārā. 29.

Your resplendency persists across all Times; in all the four *Yugas*, your fame illumines throughout the universe.

~~~

साधु संत के तुम रखवारे । असुर निकंदन राम दुलारे ॥
sādhu saṁta ke tuma rakhavāre, asura nikaṁdana rāma dulāre. 30.

You—dear-most (son) of Rāma—are the guardian of the saintly, virtuous, wise; and you are the destroyer of the fiends and the vile.

~~~

अष्ट सिद्धि नव निधि के दाता । अस बर दीन्ह जानकी माता ॥
aṣṭa siddhi nava nidhi ke dātā, asa bara dīnha jānakī mātā. 31.

You are the bestower of all eight *Siddhis* and nine *Nidhis*—Mother Sītā, daughter of Janak, herself endowed you with that power.

~~~

राम रसायन तुम्हरे पासा । सदा रहउ रघुपति के दासा ॥
rāma rasāyana tumhare pāsā, sadā rahau raghupati ke dāsā. 32.

You own the sweet treasure of devotion towards Shri Rāma; you ever abide as the foremost attendant of that Jewel of Raghu scion.

~~~

तुम्हरे भजन राम को पावै । जनम जनम के दुख बिसरावै ॥
tumhare bhajana rāma ko pāvai, janama janama ke dukha bisarāvai. 33.

अंत काल रघुबर पुर जाई । जहाँ जन्म हरिभक्त कहाई ॥
aṁta kāla raghubara pura jāī, jahām̐ janma haribhakta kahāī. 34.

Through devotion to you, one is able to obtain to the Lord; and the adversities and afflictions of millions of births become defeated thereupon; and at the time of their end, one goes to Rāma's own abode—remaining there eternally as Rāma's very own.

~~~

और देवता चित्त न धरई । हनुमत सेइ सर्ब सुख करई ॥
aura devatā citta na dharaī, hanumata sei sarba sukha karaī. 35.

Swearing by no other god and just serving Shrī Hanumān alone—one obtains every felicity in this world and the next.

~~~

संकट कटै मिटै सब पीरा । जो सुमिरै हनुमत बलबीरा ॥
saṁkaṭa kaṭai miṭai saba pīrā, jo sumirai hanumata balabīrā. 36.

All troubles are cut short, all pains removed—for those who meditate upon Shri Hanumān, the mighty, brave, supreme.

~~~

जय जय जय हनुमान गोसाईं । कृपा करहु गुरु देव की नाईं ॥
jaya jaya jaya hanumāna gosāīṁ, kṛpā karahu guru deva kī nāīṁ. 37.

Victory to you O Hanumān, O master of senses. May you remain ever victorious, ever triumphant. And do plese shower your grace upon us—as lovingly as a Guru does.

~~~

यह शत बार पाठ कर जोई | छूटै बंदि महा सुख सोई ||
yaha śata bāra pāṭha kara joī, chūṭai baṁdi mahā sukha soī. 38.

One who recites this Hanumān Chālīsā a hundred times is released from all bondages and obtains bliss everlasting.

~~

जो यह पढ़ै हनुमान चालीसा | होय सिद्धि साखी गौरीसा ||
jo yaha paṛhai hanumāna cālīsā, hoya siddhi sākhī gaurīsā. 39.

One who reads this Hanumān Chālīsā becomes a *Siddha (*Master*)*—Gaurī's Lord Shiva himself bears witness to that.

~~

तुलसीदास सदा हरि चेरा | कीजै नाथ हृदय महँ डेरा ||
tulasī-dāsa sadā hari cerā, kījai nātha hṛdaya maham ḍerā. 40.

Tulsīdās is ever a humble disciple of Shrī Rāma; O Lord Hanumān, do please take up thy abode in my heart as well (since Rāma is already there).

※

दोहा - dohā

पवन तनय संकट हरन मंगल मूरति रूप |
pavana tanaya saṁkaṭa harana maṁgala mūrati rūpa,

राम लखन सीता सहित हृदय बसहु सुर भूप ||
rāma lakhana sītā sahita hṛdaya basahu sura bhūpa.

O Son-of-Wind—O remover of all disasters and sins—O Radiant-One of the most auspicious visage—may you ever and ever abide in my heart—along with Sītā, Lakshman, Rāma—O first amongst the gods.

※ ※ ※ ※ ※

---

* The distance to Sun (**Bhānū**) is being given out in the 18th Chaupai as 96 million miles (12,000x1000x8). **Juga** (which equal 12,000 Divine-Years as per Vedic-Time-Scale) is used as a number here; **sahastra** means 1000; **jojana** is a distance of 8 miles. This distance to Sun—which is within 3.3% of modern day calculations—in mere three simple words (**juga sahastra jojana**), given out by Tulsīdās from sixteenth century India, is remarkable; for it not only shows what all our ancients knew way, way back; but it also demonstrates Tulsīdās' dexterity in choosing the right succinct words throughout his poesy.

(Author of this Original Devanāgri Hymn is: Goswamī Tulsīdās [16th Century Saint].   Translator: Sushma)

❈❈❈❈

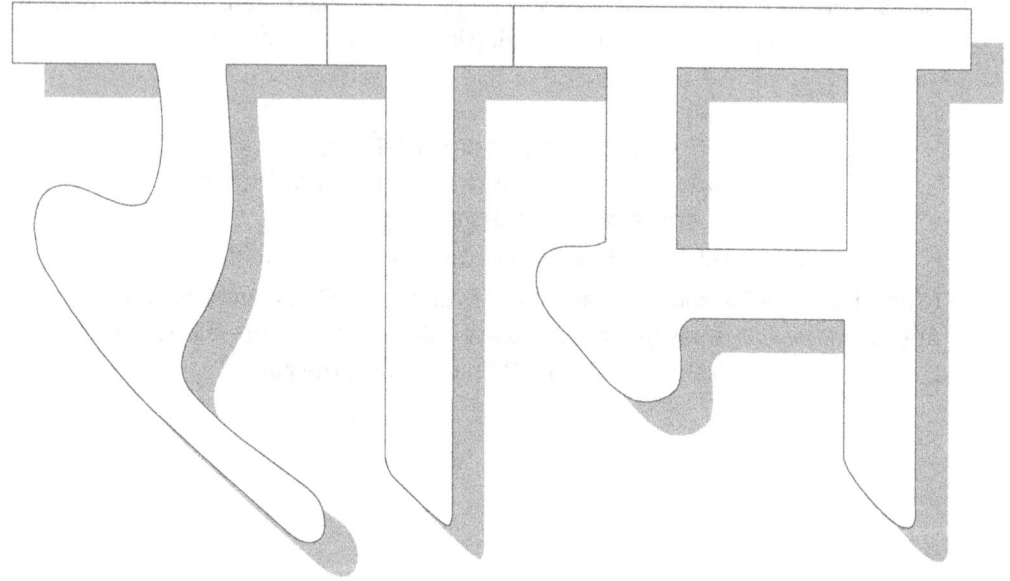

❈❈❈❈

www.ingramcontent.com/pod-product-compliance
Lightning Source LLC
Chambersburg PA
CBHW051754100526
44591CB00017B/2693